Henry C. R Becher

A trip to Mexico

being notes of a journey from Lake Erie to Lake Tezcuco and back, with an appendix, containing and being a paper about the ancient nations and races who inhabited Mexico before and at the time of the Spanish conquest

Henry C. R Becher

A trip to Mexico
being notes of a journey from Lake Erie to Lake Tezcuco and back, with an appendix, containing and being a paper about the ancient nations and races who inhabited Mexico before and at the time of the Spanish conquest

ISBN/EAN: 9783744745512

Printed in Europe, USA, Canada, Australia, Japan

Cover: Foto ©Andreas Hilbeck / pixelio.de

More available books at **www.hansebooks.com**

A TRIP TO MEXICO,

BEING

NOTES OF A JOURNEY FROM LAKE ERIE TO LAKE TEZCUCO AND BACK,

WITH

AN APPENDIX,

CONTAINING AND BEING A PAPER ABOUT THE ANCIENT NATIONS AND
RACES WHO INHABITED MEXICO BEFORE AND AT THE TIME
OF THE SPANISH CONQUEST, AND THE ANCIENT STONE
AND OTHER STRUCTURES AND RUINS OF
ANCIENT CITIES FOUND THERE.

BY

H. C. R. BECHER,

OF OSGOODE HALL, BARRISTER-AT-LAW AND Q.C.

Toronto:
WILLING AND WILLIAMSON.
MDCCCLXXX.

Entered according to Act of Parliament of Canada, in the year one thousand eight hundred and seventy-nine, by HENRY C. R. BECHER, of the City of London, in the Province of Ontario, in the Office of the Minister of Agriculture.

PREFACE.

THE reasons for publishing the "TRIP TO MEXICO" are already given.

The information about Señor Melgar and his discoveries, the possession and study of the large photographs, and a seeming absence of general information as to the ancient peoples and monuments of Mexico, have together induced the writing and publication of the Appendix; its subjects having for many years been familiar and interesting to me. What it describes, for the most part necessarily comes from other minds: often the very language of the writer is used.

It will, it is hoped, be considered as not out of place, and will give the reader a correct idea of the subjects on which it purports to treat.

Its publication has been delayed in the hope

that the Right Reverend Dr. Riley, who has been consecrated the Bishop of the Valley of Mexico, would contribute to its pages, as to the state of his church, &c., but his continued absence on the other side of the Atlantic prevents this. I am indebted to him for the likeness of President Diaz.

I have to thank Messrs. Kilburn Brothers, of Littleton, N. H., for permission to copy their photographs, the pyramid of Cholula, and the volcanoes of Popocatapetl and Iztaccihuatl; and Messrs. Harper Brothers, of New York, for their permission to copy engravings in Stephens' books, which I have only availed myself of as to the hieroglyphics at p. 176.

I have copied also M. De Waldeck's tower at Palenque, and Humboldt's pyramid at Cholula, which appear as photographs in the book. With these exceptions, and that of the heads at p. 44, which are copied from the originals, all the photographs are taken from photographs or prints brought with me from Mexico.

ERRATA.

At page 60, for Barrow, read Borrow.
At page 117, for monolinth, read monolith.
Add, Of the height given, the *cofre* is 134 feet.
At page 124, for sapilotes, read sopilotes.

TABLE OF CONTENTS

OF THE LETTERS AND THEIR NOTES.

	PAGE
INTRODUCTORY..	1–6

LETTER No. 1. Start from home—New Orleans—Mardi-Gras—Lake Pontchartrain— Leave for Vera Cruz — Opera troupe—At sea—Tampico—Tuxpan—Vera Cruz—Railway time table—Railway fares and map 6–19

LETTER No. 2. Railway train—Guard of soldiers — Departure from Vera Cruz—Railway scenery—Cordoba—Barranca de Metlac—Arrival at Orizaba—A Journey to a water-fall — A Sugar manufactory and a garden — The volcano's old name—Scan mag—Description and area of Mexico—Its volcanoes—Climate—Toltecs and Aztecs—Outlines of Mexican history 19–38

LETTER No. 3. Leave Orizaba—Railway scenery—Out of the torrid and within a temperate zone by altitude—Sight of the volcano of Orizaba at last—Boca del Monte—Table land—Malintzi — Pulque and the maguey plant—Hua

TABLE OF CONTENTS.

                                                                         PAGE

mantla—Volcanoes of Popocatapetl and Iztaccihuatl—Apizaco—Plains of Otumba—Pyramids of San Juan Teotihuacan—Prescott's account of them—Madame Calderon's mental vision—Arrival on the shores of lake Tezcuco, and in the city of Mexico 39–50

LETTER No. 4. City of Mexico—Canals filled up—Receding of lakes—Pronunciation of the names of the volcanoes, &c.—The streets—The cathedral and where it stands—Aztec calendar stone—Great teocali, and the human sacrifices—Pocket-picking, Borrow's Zincali—Guadalupe—Its cathedral—The Guardian Saint of Mexico—Santa Maria del Pillar, Santa M. del Neve, Santa M. de los Remedios—Notes—School of art—Of mines—The Museum—Sacrificial stone and god of war there—What Cortés saw in the chapels on the teocali—The old market—Streets again—The Alameda—The Paseo—The Caballero, carriages, and people—Tacubeya—Chapultepec—View from it—Plaza de toros—The Empress's Drive—Tlanetantla—Foundry for arms—Military college—Rarefied atmosphere and its effects....................... 51–74

LETTER No. 5. Expedition on the canal—Old church built by Cortés—Ixtacalco—Condition of numbers of churches—Skulls, &c., in the church-yard—Lakes Chalco and Tezcuco—Hunt for the steamer—The Palace—Hall of the ambassadors—Presented to the President—Austrian Prince Salm Salm's account of him—The Empress Carlotta's rooms—Arms that killed two Emperors—Popocatapetl—Religious toleration—Protestant missionaries—Native silversmiths—Extract from Madame Calderon—Scrap of T——'s writing—Opals..................... 50–92

LETTER No 6. Leave city of Mexico for Puebla —Arrival—Hotel de Diligentias—The cathedral, &c.—Puebla de los Angelos—Onyx marble—Cholula—The great pyra-

TABLE OF CONTENTS.

PAGE

mid—Prescott's account of it, and its temple—The Public square—Churches—Return to Puebla—Leave it for Orizaba—Arrival and departure from there—Cordoba—Arrival at Vera Cruz—Its schools, library, &c.—State of Vera Cruz, education, &c. 92–107

LETTER No. 7. Leave Vera Cruz for Jalapa—Locomotive to Paso de San Juan—Heat—Thence a mule tramway —The superintendent—Rinconada to breakfast—Plan del Rio—Hacienda and palace of Santa Anna—His character and death—Orizaba—The Cofre de Perote—Arrival at Jalapa—Village of Coatepec—Cofre de Perote—The convent and cathedral at Jalapa—The market—Serapes, rebosas, and tilmas described—Feathers and wax-work —Rainfall at Jalapa—Balconies and courtship among the Mexicans—Leave Jalapa—The Volcano of Orizaba again —Arrival at Vera Cruz—A carriage—Sopilotes—Cleanliness of Vera Cruz—Hotel de Mexico—El vomito, or drunkenness, which?—Arrival on board the steamship .. 107–126

LETTER No. 8. A norther—The situation of the ships in harbour, and the shoals—The Captain of a U. S. Frigate and his Surgeon visit us—The Battle of Dorking—Savant in Vera Cruz described—Maximilian had photos. of ruins taken—American consul at Vera Cruz has them—Visit to the consul—The photos.—Senor J. M. Melgar—Letter to Mr. Baldwin—Letter of Dr. Trowbridge, as to Senor Melgar, in notes—Return to ship—We sail for New Orleans—Catching of sharks—Robbery and brigandage in Mexico—Arrival at New Orleans—Return home 126–141

A TRIP TO MEXICO.

BEING NOTES OF A JOURNEY FROM LAKE ERIE TO LAKE TEZCUCO AND BACK.

INTRODUCTORY.

ABOUT the middle of February, those who are old or out of health have had enough of a Canadian Winter, wish for the warmth of sunshine and the gladness of green trees, and if they can, migrate in search of them. Where to go is often hard to decide. Florida has been much sought after, but we doubt whether anyone ever goes there a second time. We know it as a snare, a delusion, puffed for the benefit of hotel-keepers, steamboats and railways, a swamp, with a base of sand washed up from the sea.

Fernandina, Jacksonville and St. Augustine have

generally their yellow fever cases in the summer months, each eagerly declaring that the fever comes from the others; the heat however, is moderate, and the air balmy in winter; oranges grow there, a fact always brought out strongly; the climate is considered to be good for people with weak lungs; if it be so, we venture to think it is at the expense of their livers. Crowds go there however, and try hard to admire the country, the " beautiful river St. John," and, more than all, the "ancient Spanish city of St. Augustine," with its "ancient fort," " ancient cathedral " and " ancient gate."

All these things, as described by the flowing pen of Mrs. Harriet Beecher Stowe and other writers, attract shoals of people who are well in health, as also those who are not. Would that that lady had had as much charity for the memory of a great English poet as she has shewn for St. Augustine in her glowing description of it!

The Ancient Spanish city is a village mostly of small modern wooden houses, built on a sand-bank, surrounded on the land side by stunted pines and a swamp, through which the railway reaches it from the St. John, while on the sea-side all view is shut out by a long sand-bank island with no speck of vegetation on it, lying along and within a stone's throw of the coast: the ancient cathedral is in shape a large barn, with big square windows in its sides and ends, and at one end something to hang three little bells in. The ancient gate consists of its two posts, and the ancient fort is a little stone thing in the orthodox shape of forts of a hundred years or so ago, not worth crossing the deep sandy road to see, unless you have never seen a fort before.

We had nearly forgotten there was a "plaza," which consists of an acre of sand ancle deep, with half a dozen handsome trees: but one good thing in St. Augustine must be noted, and that is, its yacht club-house, (we don't think there were any yachts) whose members, if you are a gentleman, will offer you the hospitality of their reading room, a kindness you cannot fail to be thankful for.

But if you want to shoot alligators, *go to Florida*; of all places, *there* they abound; your bags will be certain and many up the river Ocklawa-ha, a tributary of the St. John. The storekeepers of the cities have infant alligators captured and sent to them from this river for the admiration and purchase of tourists from the north. Well we recollect a young lady of our party at Jacksonville, looking at half a tubful of these abominable little reptiles crunching and rattling over each other, addressing them as "*dear little things!*"

Bermuda has a delightful winter climate, and is cheaply and quickly accessible from New York; and Augusta in Georgia, and many other Southern places of winter resort in the United States have their advantages, but those we have seen fall sadly short of the puffs given to them, and many are cold and damp.

St. Augustine was so much so last January, that an invalid Canadian judge left it for Nassau, New Providence, where he found a warm dry climate, a comfortable hotel, and moderate charges.

Thirty years ago, we read for the first time Prescott's charming history of the Conquest of Mexico, and ever since had strongly desired to visit the land and the descendants of the people, he so beautifully describes. This desire became much stronger during the early part of last winter. How much better it would be, we thought, to go to that wonderful country for a winter outing, than in the beaten track with its greater expenses and insipidity.

But many grave considerations were involved: probable "Northers," the terror of navigators in the Gulf of Mexico; possible yellow fever at Vera Cruz; and, more than all, was Mexico a country to take ladies to, and to travel about with? for we are *tête de famille*, and however valiant we might be on our own account, we had no right to be so for those belonging to us. We made many enquiries: one gentleman wrote us from New York, "people here laugh at the idea of taking ladies to Mexico;" but the Rev. Dr. Riley, the newly elected Protestant Bishop of Mexico, set our doubts at rest, encouraged our going, gave us good advice and letters, for all which kindnesses we shall ever feel deeply indebted to him.

And so it came to pass that our party, consisting of four ladies and one gentleman, left their home in a city of Western Ontario, not far from the shores of Lake Erie, on the 11th February, 1878, intent upon getting to Mexico and half way and more across the continent, and seeing as much of the country and its people as a stay of five or six weeks would allow them.

One of our party wrote letters containing a sort of diary describing our tour for the amusement of a relative in England, who thinks they would be as interesting to many readers as they were to herself, and wishes to see them in print; for this reason and in the hope that they may, at all events, interest the many Canadians who go "South" to avoid the cold of our winter, or, what is worse, that of the early spring, they are offered for publication, with some additions omitted in the haste of their first writing, and here they begin :—

Letter No. 1.

STEAMSHIP CITY OF MEXICO,
GULF OF MEXICO, 18th Feb., 1878.

MY DEAR A,—We left Thornwood on Monday last the 11th, driving to the station well covered up in a sleigh; such a bright beautiful day, the thermometer at zero and the snow lying deep everywhere!

We went out of Ontario by Amherstburg at the N.W. corner of Lake Erie, where the river Detroit flows into it; at six the next morning we were in Cincinnati Ohio, at noon in Louisville Kentucky, and there we stayed till midnight. Both these places are beautiful cities on the river Ohio, surrounded by a lovely and thickly settled country.

Getting to and exploring the great Mammoth Cave of Kentucky employed us from Tuesday night till early Thursday morning, when we left Cave City, breakfasting at Nashville in Tennessee, and dining at Montgomery in Alabama: our Pullman had but few occupants and was very comfortable.

On Friday morning at 8 o'clock we awoke close to New Orleans: it was summer; on either side of the railway brush palms, magnolias, and live oak were growing in abundance; and, arrived at the St. Charles Hotel, a bouquet of roses and many flowers graced our breakfast table. What a change of scene and temperature (seventy degrees of Fahrenheit and more), between Canada and Monday, and New Orleans and Friday! and, but for loitering on the way, we might have been here on Wednesday.

We were told an opera troupe was going to Vera Cruz, and that every berth in the ship was engaged; but three of the best state rooms we afterwards found were to be had, and we quickly secured them, having half an hour before almost given up all hope of going at all; for there was no other ship for three weeks, and that delay would have brought us to Vera Cruz on our return, at a much later time than was prudent to be there. Passage money (one hundred dollars each, to Vera Cruz *and return*) paid, there were nearly two days in which to get ready, and see something of New Orleans; but then came pressing on me the fact that Spanish was *the* language of Mexico, and that though I believed *Señor* and *Señora* and *olla-podrida* were Spanish, and that C—— and A—— and L—— had studied hard at the language while we stopped at the St. Thomas station and at intervals since, still, all this might not be enough ; so we determined to get an interpreter if we could, who would not only save us from all trouble on the score of language, but who knew something of the country, and who would take care of us generally.

So an advertisement was put in the "Picayune" which produced about a hundred applicants of all colours, driving the clerks in the St. Charles office nearly wild ; but only six or seven of them were permitted to see us ; from them we selected one, whose testimonials are undoubted, and who is just what we want.

We were so sorry not to be able to wait for the carnival, for New Orleans now out-does the world in carnival making. There was a mock proclamation in all the city papers from King Mardi Gras to all his loving subjects, commanding what is to be done on Shrove Tuesday.

I have said *mock* proclamation, but no document of that kind from King or Kaiser has been more fully obeyed, than will be this of King "Mardi Gras." All business will be suspended ; every thoroughfare and public place in New Orleans will be given up to grave, costly masquerading, mummery, and clever tom-foolery during the whole day, and elements of all these will pervade the many balls, parties, and places of public amusement at its close.

We were sorry to leave New Orleans so soon on its own account, there is so much to see and admire in it; it is a new and an old, a French and an American city in one; we must manage to see more of it on our return.

But Lake Pontchartrain was a disappointment;— a melancholy sheet of water with trees on invisible banks (so low are they), a light-house and three or four little wooden restaurants, where New Orleans eats fish dinners, and gets fresh air.

What a tired lot we were when we went to our beds on Saturday night! but we had done all we had to do and were quite ready for our move to the ship, and yesterday morning by eight o'clock we were all on board bag and baggage, and soon steaming down the great Mississippi towards the Gulf of Mexico, about a hundred miles distant. We passed the mouth of the river early in the evening, and to-day, as I write, we are about one hundred and eighty miles S.W. of it, on our course for Tampico, the first Mexican port we touch at, and which we expect to reach about daylight on Wednesday; then comes

Tuxpan; and on Friday morning, all going well, we are to be at Vera Cruz.

The Gulf is as calm as can be desired, and nearly as blue as the Bay of Naples in its best mood. We like our ship, our captain, our purser, *almost* like the whole opera troupe, who appear everywhere, but we *rather* wish they didn't smoke *quite* so much and hadn't *quite* so many dogs.

Have they heard, we wonder, of that troupe travelling in Mexico not many years since who were robbed and stripped, and whose prima donna perched on a rock, was made to sing her best for the amusement of their robbers.

We have just passed large patches of muddy water in a space of about two miles in this deep bright blue sea, which cause some speculation among the passengers; one, whose nationality is settled at once, suggests that the big fishes, &c., are holding a democratic meeting, far down below; the captain says when he passed here last, there were patches of petroleum on the water; my conclusion is, volcanic disturbances.

The weather is delicious to us, coming as we do from frost and snow; there is a gentle breeze, a summer sun; we are steaming with sails up rapidly through the water, and there are no end of Portuguese men of war with their tiny sails up, scudding with us; it is so amusing to see these little creatures when the wind is too strong for them, trying *not* to upset; and if they do upset to see how cannily they get up into the wind, hoist their sail again and speed on. The air is soft, the thermometer 73°, in my state room on deck now, at four o'clock, and all our present world seems to point to dreaminess and rest; certainly if there ever is any rest or comfort in a sea voyage it is at its commencement. The awful packings up, and land-journeys, and letter-writing, and looking after baggage, and the rushes for train and ship —all are over; nothing can now be left behind, and we have only to be quiet and rest.

Wednesday, 20th Feb.

We are well south of the tropic of Cancer, and about noon anchor outside the bar of the river off Tampico, which is distant seven miles. The captain of the little steamer visiting us fears a "Norther," and thinks he may not be able to get back before it comes, so we don't go to Tampico, much as we desire to see it. We have had a gale from the S.E. since Monday and C—— and A—— and L—— have suffered much from sea sickness; T—— as usual, is as placid and undisturbed as the captain of the ship, but now the weather seems well enough, though they *will* promise the "Norther." It is very hot, and myriads of beautifully coloured winged beetles and flies come on board while we are at anchor; parrots and other bright plumaged birds are brought on board for sale.

THURSDAY, 21st Feb.

We left our anchorage about seven last evening, and this morning at eight are anchored off Tuxpan. We passed on our left the "Havana," a fine steamer of this line (the Alexandre of N. York), lying fast on a coral reef, on which she ran and became a wreck last July.

The land is high behind and about Tuxpan, and we see hills, seemingly of volcanic origin far inland. Tuxpan is visible across the bar, a few short miles up the river, but we cannot land, for the "Norther" may come yet, and thus these two Mexican ports are lost to us, and become annoyances, for we *must* stop for freight, and so lose much time.

There are no harbours, and no lights along the coast; the Alexandre company, we hear, offered to place lights on the bars of both the Tampico and Tuxpan rivers, and keep them alight on and about the days they would be required for their steamers, and advertise them, if the Mexican government would do the rest.

The matter was discussed in Congress, one of whose members proposed to dispose of the question by the enactment of a law prohibiting steamers from running at night at all! There are no lights.

To-morrow morning we are to get to Vera Cruz, and if we are up very early, and it is clear, we shall see Orizaba, called by sailors the "Star of the Seas," from its glistening peak—a respectable mountain, more than two thousand feet higher than Mont Blanc.

FRIDAY, 22nd Feb., 8 A.M.

Here we are at anchor in the harbour of Vera Cruz, if a poor anchorage between three shoals can be called a harbour. Orizaba was hidden in the clouds, and we missed the approach to this place, in ignominious sleep. Close on our right is the famed castle of San Juan d'Ulloa; above it and behind, and to our left, shoals, coral reefs, surf; in front of us the long sea wall, the mole, and the city of the True Cross, looking so bright and clean, and strange and pretty and foreign!

We soon land at the mole, pass the custom house close by, with little trouble, and cross a large square crowded with mule-carts, Indians and Negroes

VERA CRUZ.

Castle of San Juan d'Ulloa to the left.

moving freight from, or to the mole, and are soon housed in the Hotel de Mexico. The bed-rooms are after the fashion of the East; a narrow iron bedstead, no drapery save musquito curtains, a couple of chairs and a washing stand form the whole furniture, and the floor is of brick. The building is three stories high, and the halls and passages from the ground-floor to the attic, have, instead of floors, iron rods or gratings across them to permit the circulation of air; this makes walking about the house unpleasant for people who are given to giddiness or not sure-footed.

Vera Cruz is soon seen, and one soon tires of seeing it; the streets are narrow, the houses flat-roofed, and for the most part low; but then there is the great square, the Plaza de la Constitution, with its beautiful tropical trees and plants, and there is a fine old church, and the Governor's palace. Each street has a gutter trickling down its middle, dosed daily with disinfectants, and there is an army of buzzards, the scavengers of the place, who perch themselves everywhere and anywhere. The eating and drinking part of our hotel, the restaurant, is at its base, and a distinct ownership, mine host of the hotel having nothing to do with it; this is, we hear, the hotel custom all over the country.

We went to the railway station, to which, and a little beyond it, is a very unnecessary tram or street railway, for you can walk through the city in ten minutes.* The railway station seems all that can be desired : outside it and outside the sea wall, is an excellent wharf, built by the railway company, in fulfilment, we were told, of their agreement with the government, and at a large expense.

Its use to the company and to the public would be of great value, but it must not be ! There is a large number of men and mules whose constant employment is, and long has been, to take freight from the mole all round to the railway, and from the railway all round to the mole, and if the new wharf is used, all this work would be stopped, and the men would PRONOUNCE ! But this is none of my business, which has been to find the railway time-table, and here it is, minus the mixed and pulque trains :—

---

* We afterwards found this was part of the tramroad to Medellin, so named after the town Cortes was born in.

Estaciones. (Stations.)	DISTANCIAS. kilómetros. (kilometres.)	millas inglesas. (English miles.)	TRAIN TO MEXICO.
			noche.
Vera Cruz			12 00
Tejería	15½	9½	12 45
Soledad	42	26	1 45
Camaron	63¼	39¼	2 45
Paso del Macho	76	47¼	3 15
Paso del Macho	76	47¼	3 30
Atoyac	86	53½	4 00
Córdova	105¾	65¾	4 55
Fortin	113¾	70¾	5 30
Orizaba	132	82	6 20
Orizaba	132	82	6 35
Encinal	142½	88½	
Maltrata	152¼	94½	7 30
Bota	157¼	97½	
Alta Luz	165¾	103	
Boca del Monte	172½	107¼	9 00
Boca del Monte	172½	107¼	9 40
San Andrés	203¼	126¼	10 40
Rinconada	223¾	139	11 15
San Màrcos	241¾	150¼	11 50
Huamantla	259	161	12 30
Apizaco	281½	176¾	1 20
Apizaco	284½	176¾	1 50
Guadalupe (hacienda)	299¾	186¼	2 30
Soltepec	311½	192½	3 00
Apam	331	205¾	3 40
Irolo	346½	215½	4 10
Ometusco	356¼	221¼	4 35
La Palma	362½	225¼	4 50
Otumba	368½	229	5 05
San Juan Teotihuacan	380	236	5 25
Tepexpan	391¼	243	5 50
Mexico	423¾	263¼	6 50

Trenes a Puebla.

Estaciones.	Distancias en kilómts.	Distancias en mls. ing.	TREN DE MEXICO	TREN DE VERA CRUZ.
			mana.	tarde.
APIZACO			5 30	1 55
Santa-Ana	16¾	10½	6 10	2 35
Panzacola	35	12¾	6 50	3 15
PUEBLA	47	29¼	7 20	3 45

To get to Puebla we shall have to come back to Apizaco, from whence there is a branch railway—time, about two hours to Puebla.

The railway fare, first class to Mexico is sixteen dollars; second, twelve; third, eight dollars; about thirty pounds of luggage is allowed free: beyond this we were charged about as we should be in Italy.

I send you a tiny map of the railway, shewing the country, towns, lakes, and mountains about it; the railway laid down on it to Jalapa, however, is only a railway *proper* to San Juan, eighteen miles out from Vera Cruz; beyond that, it is worked by mules.

As far as the eye can reach, Vera Cruz is surrounded on the land side by a barren deep sandy plain; a few miles along the coast to the south however, a tramway takes you to an oasis, a place called Medellin, where a river flows into the gulf and makes a watering, gambling, dancing, holiday resort for Vera Cruzans in the season, which is not now.

We did not go there; indeed my great desire in coming to Vera Cruz is to get out of it and its neighbourhood as quickly as possible, for the reason that there is never a certainty that yellow fever is not

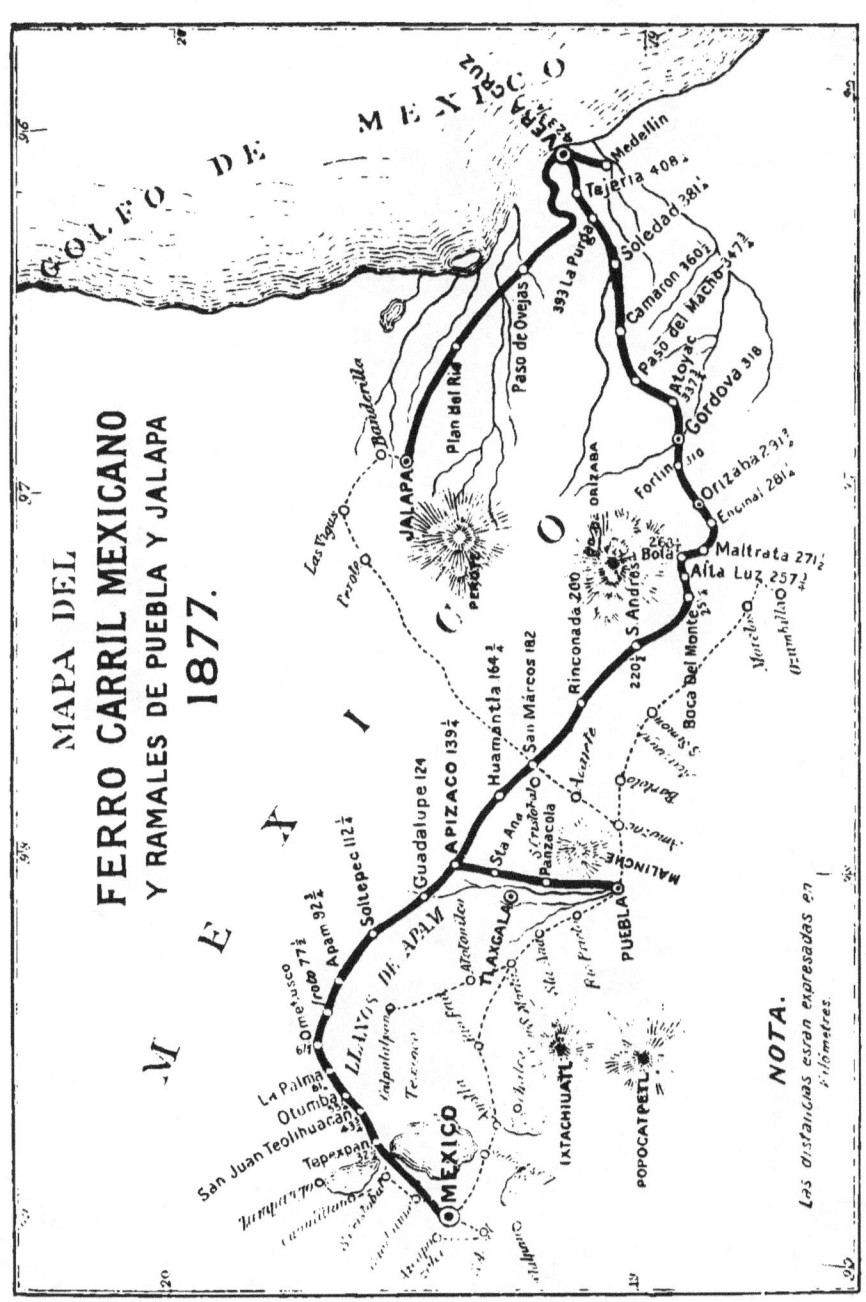

present; but Vera Cruzans laugh at one's fears of fever. You shall hear more of Vera Cruz on our return to it.

The heat is oppressive, the air close, we are impatient for the night and the train that is to take us up into the mountains, and to a fresher, purer atmosphere. My next letter will be from somewhere between this and the great table land, more probably from the ancient city of Mexico.

Letter No. 2.

Hotel de Diligentias, Orizaba, 23rd February, 1878.

IN Mexico, every passenger train carries soldiers to guard it, and when we got to the station last night, there were some twenty-five men mustered to come with us, small, lithe, wiry Aztecs, their uniform more French than anything else: each man with his *serape* striped in many bright colours, and so carrying it, or wrapped in it, as to make himself a striking picture to new comers. The whole squad, as they stood at ease on the platform, chatting and smoking, waiting for the order to get into their appointed carriages, with the strong gas-light gleaming upon their arms and accoutrements, made up a group not easily to be forgotten.

The first-class carriages are English, and we had one to ourselves, wishing in vain for a Pullman: we left punctually at midnight, and just then came the "Norther," so long threatened on board the ship: the gale was very hard, and the effect was to fill the air with clouds of sand from the desert we were passing over, a good deal of it finding its way somehow into the carriage, though the windows were all closed. In a couple of hours we were out of it, protected as we supposed by higher land, for we could see nothing. The night became close and hot, the air laden with perfumes from blossom or leaf invisible to us, which at intervals were so powerfully sweet as to be oppressive: how we longed to see what we were passing as the train took us continually upwards! We could now and then make out the figure of a tall palm against the sky, or we thought we could, which did as well. About five in the morning we arrived at the Cordoba station; still all is darkness; Indian women bring us tortillas and strange fruits, and oranges, bananas, and pineapples at infinitesimal prices. We go on; the train seems to descend, and soon we are at the next station, Fortin, which is on the left bank of the barranca de Metlac: barranca means a ravine, or I should say, according to our ideas of ravines, a great many of them put into one. Day has dawned; we run along the precipice forming the side of the barranca. Far below at its bottom is a silver ribbon, the river; rock, and rich rank vegetation are above, below, on all sides of us. We run through tunnels to come out upon ledges, overhanging more precipices, till all of a sudden the train is on what we are told is the great Metlac viaduct. We are all on our feet, astonished, almost alarmed: We seem to be on stilts high up in the air. Suddenly, quietly, the train turns to the right, crossing the barranca on a curve, which takes it to the opposite side, *turned to the right about.* We are soon off the viaduct, running along more ledges and through tunnels on the side of the barranca opposite to the one we have left, but in the same direction from which we came. We catch our breath: it has all been very grand, very startling, but it is over, and we are out of the barranca (whose greatest width is 900 feet, depth 375 feet) and with broader daylight enter upon the valley of Sumidero, wherein is the City of Orizaba, the ancient Ahaulizapan. And now our conversation becomes interjectional; the scene before us seems a work of enchantment, so suddenly does it appear to us, and so strangely and perfectly beautiful is it. Beyond and about us is an immense undulating plain surrounded by lofty mountains, and here and there so narrowed by them, as almost to be lost, but coming out wider in the far distance, to be nearly lost again, and at last completely shut in : everywhere are to be seen brilliant varying shades of green, here and there houses, churches, odd-looking buildings, and always in the moving foreground the rich foliage of tropical trees and shrubs : add to this the brightest, loveliest early morning that ever shone, and there is a scene that, while it somewhat bewildered, charmed the sight and senses of the party who, but twelve short days before, were shut up amid ice and snow, where no green leaf was to be seen. The train now runs swiftly, and we are soon at the Orizaba station. Some excellent coffee and a roll, and we get into an elderly ricketty carriage, drawn by a pair of mules, on our way to the town : a drive of a mile brings us into the long principal street : the houses are good and of stone ; the lower windows are protected by projecting iron bars, forming a sort of cage outside the embrasure, Spanish fashion, and from within them dark-eyed women and children gaze at us as we pass. We are soon established in our rooms and attain baths, cleanliness and rest. Orizaba is named after the great volcano, some 25 miles distant from it : it has twenty-two thousand inhabitants, many churches, some manufactories of cotton, and coarse cloth, a high, and many other schools, and a river : it is very picturesque, is well built, and is about four thousand feet above the sea. It has, it is said, a delightful climate all the year round, a happy medium between the abominable hot lands below, and the perhaps too rarified air of the table land above.

Taking a late breakfast, we are agreeably surprised at meeting the Hon. Mr. de S— and Mr. G—: they are going to see a waterfall, a sugar mill, and a wonderful garden, and want us to go too; the first I object to, as taking Canadians to see a waterfall seems like taking Newcastle people to see coals : but we go, and are so glad we did, though the waterfall is four or five miles off. I send you a photograph of it, but it can give you no idea of its beauty : it is a series of bright thick cascades jumping and foaming from beneath a heavy fringe of tropical foliage, and tumbling down a rocky bank, dotted with lichens, maiden hair and other ferns. In front of it is a lovely little woody glen with the rapid stream from the fall rushing through it. We have looked in vain for Orizaba ; he is too high to be seen always with the commonalty of mountains, and we must wait patiently for some clearness in his high atmosphere. We next visited the sugar manufactory, and were obligingly shown all over it. We saw the whole process from the cane going in at one end, to the sugar loaf coming out at the other. And then we drove to the garden of many acres, of Señor Maringa: there were flowers without end, those shown with the most pride, and receiving the least notice from us, being English. There were the orange, the lemon, the banana, the olive, the almond, the coffee shrub, all growing luxuriantly. I must not forget some mango-trees with the fruit just formed, almost as big as peas. I was disappointed, for I hoped to eat mangoes before leaving the country; but we were told there were plenty ripening and ripe in the hot lands below, these, their relatives, being in a much less stimulating climate.

The coffee bushes and their flowers and fruit surprised us with their beauty: but what we most admired were the hundreds of orange trees laden with delicious fruit and covered with blossoms: there was perhaps too much of their fragrance. We thought we had seen these trees in their perfection—in Sicily and Malta, but Señor Maringa's garden has undeceived us. We ate and carried off as many as we chose, and agreed that we had not *quite* known before what oranges were.

On our return from a drive of ten miles or so, I took L— to see the inside of the cathedral, which is rather tawdry : it is the first thing of the kind she has ever seen, and it does not impress her much.

In the City of Mexico we are told there is one church more imposing in its interior even than the great St. Peter's ; *nous verrons.*

Being so near the great mountain Orizaba reminds me of a shocking scandal about him, and a near lady mountain, Iztaccihuatl (the *white woman*) wife of Popocatepetl (*smoking mountain*), which I read on board the ship, in a funny English translation of a Spanish book, giving an account of the building of this railway.

The scandal was handed down from the Toltecs : Cortes must have heard it, and been pained at the state of mountain morality it indicated.

It seems from the story that Orizaba's name at the time, whenever that was, was Citlalteptl, and he, being then a much nearer neighbour flirted a good deal and very improperly with Iztaccihuatl, who, forgetting her high position, encouraged him and flirted outrageously too. Naturally, her husband did not like it, and he told her so ; but the more he didn't like it, the more she carried on, till at last Popocatepetl, following Othello's example, if Othello had lived then, and if not, from his own mere mountainous jealousy and cussedness, kills her—how, the scandal-monger does not say. Citlalteptl (which his name is now Orizaba, and that change of name is a suspicious circumstance) seems thereupon, to have run away—fancy eighteen thousand feet running away!—for the story says that "dumb with consternation, he is destroyed in his wild flight," while poor Popocatepetl becomes "a victim to remorse, and is frozen to death near the corpse of his victim, to weep over his crime eternally."

The story is a sad one, and of course it is not for me to say it is not true; but there is this strange circumstance in it, that Popocatepetl having been frozen stiff and dead, should weep eternally, or indeed weep at all. Perhaps a near view of these three parties may enable me to form a correct judgment about the whole story. I have always had a *high* opinion of the Andes (specially), and of mountains generally, and hope it is untrue.

I have been scribbling nonsense at a great rate, and now it occurs to me to be serious, and give you as shortly as I can, some account of the country and its history.

Everybody is in bed and asleep, the house is quiet. I have some notes with me, a good memory, as to much information I have been gobbling up for weeks past about Mexico; and besides, I am *in it*, so that what I tell you will have much additional importance, and enable you the better to understand my letters. Read then if you like, skip if you don't, what I am now about to write to you.

Mexico, as it now is, forms the north part of Central America; on its north lie Texas, New Mexico, Arizona, Upper California; on its west is the Pacific Ocean ; on its east the Gulf of Mexico ; on the south it is bounded by Guatemala and British Honduras.

Its area is about seven hundred and forty-four thousand square miles; its population between nine and ten millions, about one-half being pure Indians, the remainder Spanish and other European races, half-breeds, negroes, and others.

About half the country is within the limits of the temperate zone, the other between the tropics; about its centre is that vast plateau, the table land, in parts from six to eight thousand feet above the sea ; along this plain, which is formed by their expansion, runs from north-west to south-east, a lofty chain of mountains, part of the great range of the Andes.

On a fissure running across the continent, on or close to the nineteenth parallel of south latitude, are the following volcanoes, the height of which, in feet above the sea, I give from Humboldt:

Orizaba	17,879
Iztaccihuatl	15,705
Popocatepetl	17,726
Toluca	15,168
Colima	12,005
Jorullo	4,265

This last is a youthful mountain; it only came into existence in the year 1759, and was then suddenly shot up, like Jack-in-the-box, out of a "broad and long peaceful plain."

The Cofre de Perote, 13,553 feet above the sea, Humboldt does not consider a true volcano.

The tableland slopes more or less abruptly on the east to the Gulf of Mexico, on the west to the Pacific.

The Spaniards, on coming to the country, distinguished the lowlands, along the coast, as the *tierras calientes*, hot or littoral lands; the range higher up, as the *tierras templadas*, temperate lands; and the range above them again, as the *tierras frias*, cold lands; and this classification with its names is still retained.

It is easy to understand what difference of climate must follow these differences of altitude, and that the flora of Mexico must comprehend almost all the vegetable products of the world, and that (I quote Prescott), "in the course of a few hours the traveller may experience every gradation of climate, embracing torrid heat and glacial cold, and pass through different zones of vegetation, including wheat and the sugar cane, the ash and the palm, apples, olives and guavas."

The Toltecs were the first inhabitants of Mexico; they came "somewhere from the north," nobody knows where, bringing with them some degree of civilization, and possessed the country up to the end of the twelfth century, when they disappeared as mysteriously as they had come.

They had good laws and a harmless religion, and these seem to have been adopted, though much barbarized, by the Aztecs, who took possession of the country upon their departure.

The Aztecs are said to have come from the north too, but it seems more probable that both races came from another continent, for all the Indians of the north, in America, have always been savages, pure and simple, with no trace of any knowledge or art that Toltec or Aztec possessed. The Toltec never was a savage, and the Aztec only in his religion, and its frightful human sacrifices.

> "Far away
> Yuhidthiton led forth the Aztecas,
> To spread in other lands Mexitli's name,
> And rear a mightier empire, and set up
> Again their foul idolatry ; till Heaven,
> Making blind zeal and bloody avarice
> Its ministers of vengeance, sent among them
> The heroic Spaniards' unrelenting sword."
> *Southey's Madoc.*

The Aztecs founded the City of Tenochtitlan or Mexico, in the year 1325, inspired in the selection of its site by seeing an eagle on the shore of the Lake Tezcuco perched on a cactus, holding a serpent in his talons, his wings spread to the rising sun. They took this as pointing to where their future capital should be. The legend is preserved in the Arms of Mexico to the present day.

The Aztecs remained, and were the possessors of the country, under the rule of their king, Montezuma, when Cortes invaded it in 1519; their government ceased with his conquest, but they have ever since occupied the country, and are now, and have been since its separation from Spain, the governing race.

In 1540, Mexico was united with other Spanish territories, under the name of New Spain, and was governed by Spanish Viceroys until 1810, when long discontent turned into open rebellion. Iturbide, one of the later leaders of this revolution, achieved great successes over the Spaniards, and really brought about the independence of the country, and, in 1822, was proclaimed Emperor. He was, however, quite unfitted to control or reduce the anarchy that prevailed, and in 1823 abdicated, retiring to Italy, where he agreed to remain.

The divisions in Mexico induced his return in 1824, without waiting for an answer to a letter he had written to the Congress, offering his services as an officer of the government merely, in restoring order.

This letter was read in Congress, and its writer proclaimed an outlaw. Ignorant of this, he arrived at Vera Cruz, with much regal paraphernalia, was seized, and within a week shot, and "buried like a dog."

Before the departure of its first emperor, a republican form of government had been adopted upon the principle of that of the United States, and, in 1824 the independence of Mexico was recognised by all governments except those of Brazil and Spain; Brazil acknowledged its independence in 1830, Spain in 1836.

The main outlines of Mexican history since, are as follow:

1845. War with the United States commences, which terminates in 1848 by General Scott taking the City of Mexico by assault, followed by a treaty of peace, ceding to the Government of the United States, New Mexico, Upper California, and Texas, the last two lost to Mexico long before.

1853. Santa Anna, who had been more than once elected President, made Dictator.

1855. Santa Anna abdicates; Carera elected President; he abdicates, and is succeeded first by Alvarez, and afterwards by General Comonfort.

1856. Property of the clergy sequestrated.

1857. New Constitution established: Comonfort chosen President.

1858. *Coup d'état;* Constitution annulled by church party, Comonfort compelled to retire, and General Zuloaga takes the government; Benito Juarez declared Constitutional President at Vera Cruz; Civil War.

1859. General Miguel Miramon nominated President at Mexico by the Junta; Zuloaga abdicates.

1859. Juarez confiscates the church property.

1861. Miramon having been defeated, Juarez enters Mexico, is re-elected President, and made Dictator by the Congress.

" Gross outrages on foreigners in Mexico, and a partial repudiation of its debt, induce the Governments of England, France and Spain to act together towards compelling redress; Spanish troops land at Vera Cruz, and it surrenders.

1862. The British and French forces arrive at Vera Cruz.

" Project for establishing a Mexican monarchy, to be filled by the Archduke Maximilian, brother of the Emperor of Austria, disapproved of by British and Spanish Governments.

" Conference at Orizaba; the English and Spanish are satisfied and withdraw their forces; the French remain and declare war against Mexico.

1863. Juarez and his Government retire to San Luis de Potosi; City of Mexico occupied by Marshal Bazaine; General Forey, who had before appropriated both military and civil power at Vera Cruz, enters Mexico with his army.

1863. A Provisional Government is formed in the City of Mexico.

" Assembly of notables at Mexico decide on the establishment of a limited hereditary monarchy with a Roman Catholic prince as emperor, and offer the crown to the Archduke Maximilian.

1864. The Archduke having accepted the offer, lands at Vera Cruz as Emperor of Mexico, with the Empress; Oaxaca surrenders to Marshal Bazaine.

1865. The Emperor Maximilian proclaims the end of the war with France, and martial law against all armed bands of men, under which latter proclamation Juarist generals are taken prisoners and shot.

" The United States Government protests against the French occupation of Mexico.

1866. The Emperor Napoleon agrees to withdraw all his troops by November, 1867; guerilla warfare going on between the imperialist and liberal parties, and Matamoras and Tampico are taken by the latter.

1866. The Empress Carlotta leaves for France; she solicits help there in vain.

1867. Maximilian leaves the City of Mexico and at the head of his army arrives at Queretaro.

" The liberals take Queretaro by the treachery of Miguel Lopez, an officer of the imperial army; after a trial by court-martial, they shoot the Emperor Maximilian, Miramon and Mejia there.

" The City of Mexico taken by the liberals after 67 days' siege; Vera Cruz surrenders; the Republic is re-established; Santa Anna is banished; Juarez re-elected President.

1872. Juarez re-elected President; insurrection; civil war headed by Diaz, which is nearly subdued when Juarez dies; the country becomes tranquil, and Diaz accepts amnesty; Lerdo is elected President.

" Railway from Vera Cruz to Mexico completed.

1876. Lerdo is re-elected President, but there is a revolution, and on the 4th March, 1877, General Porfirio Diaz is proclaimed as his successor, and is still President of the Republic.

I have left out many names, many events, many revolutions, and countless insurrections that should appear even in my little outline, but you will be thankful for their omission. As to the revolutions, they are the usual, it would almost be fair to say the constitutional, method, of changing the Government in Mexico !

Beautiful, unhappy country, what turmoil, robbery, oppression, bloodshed, misgovernment, it has gone through since its Spanish conquerors first disturbed its peace ! If they initiated all this—and who can say they did not ?—they also brought with them Christianity, and to expound and inculcate its meaning, many of the ecclesiastics of their time, (and pious good men they were), not forgetting the Inquisition, which they established on the shores of Lake Tezcuco with a branch much enlarging its business at Puebla. But all this, and all that has followed in three centuries and a half and more, has left its people seemingly yet unfit, rightly to govern their country or themselves.

As to the gold and silver, the mines and minerals, and its other products and sources of wealth, I refer you to the geographies and cyclopædias.

You should read Madame Calderon de la Barca's charming book, again Prescott's; and there is Sir Arthur Helps' book, quite new, compared to the others.

RAILR 13 VERA CRUZ TO MEXICO

Letter No. 3.

HOTEL ITURBIDE, CITY OF MEXICO,
25th February.

WE got here last night, and as my last letter was from Orizaba, I give you the diary—much of which is addressed to you, shewing our journey here.

24th Feb.

We leave Orizaba this morning at half-past six. The most interesting and beautiful parts of this wonderful railway are between Orizaba and Boca Del Monte, before arriving at which place the stations of Encinal, Maltrata, Bota, and Alta Luz are passed. We run through the valley of Encinal, which is much higher than that of Orizaba, and enter the gorges of the Infiernillo (little hell) and Second Infiernillo; emerging from thence, the train passes into the valley and among the beautiful mountains of Maltrata, and then up and up, round and round, but always ascending, till we look down upon peaks and clouds. Often the mountain wall on one side of us is within a few feet of the carriage window, while just outside the other is a precipice of a thousand feet. We are now out of the torrid, and well within the temperate zone, not by latitude, but by *altitude;* look across the deep valley on our left: on the mountain side above it, is a forest of pines, reminding us of the land of our home. Flowers are in abundance on either side of us, and we breast the ascent so slowly, and are so close to them frequently, as to see their full forms and many shades of colour distinctly as we pass. I note here that the Fairleigh locomotive is a wonder of power and fitness for its work; without it they could not work this railway, its gradients are so steep, its curves so sharp. Soon we stop at, and pass, Alta Luz—*but look, oh look!* there at last is Orizaba—immense, calm, majestic; in shape, reminding us of Etna! The train runs faster, and attains soon something like level ground: we are (I quote Prescott) " on the summit of the cordillera of the Andes—the colossal range, that after traversing South America and the Isthmus of Darien, spreads out as it enters Mexico into that vast sheet of table land which maintains an elevation of more than six thousand feet for the distance of nearly two hundred leagues, until it gradually declines in the higher latitudes of

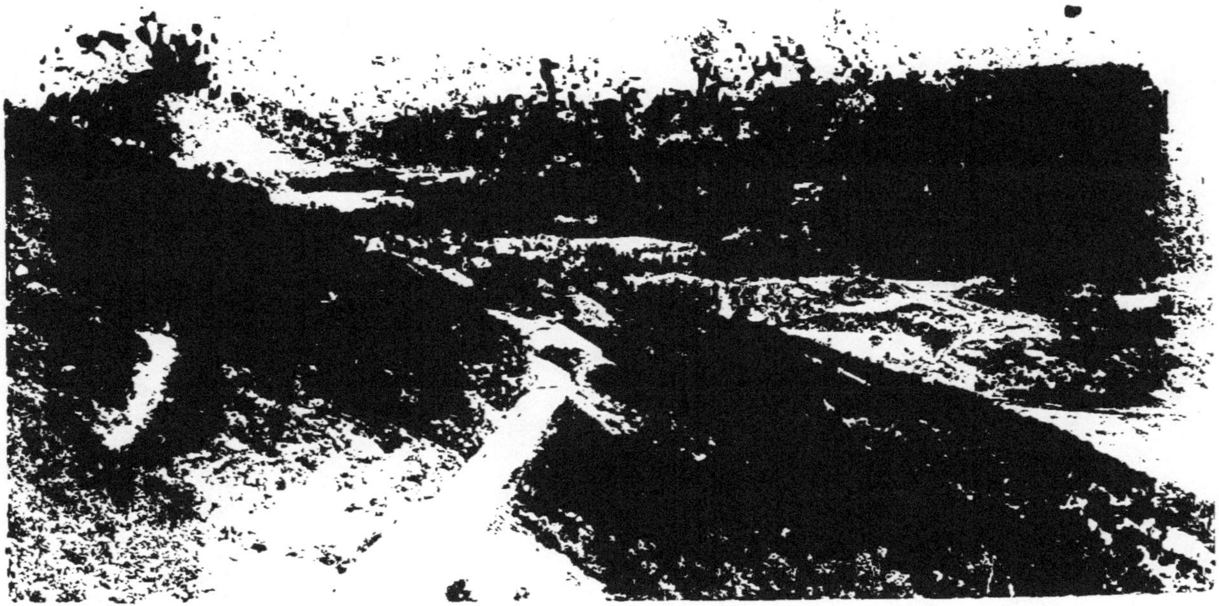

RAILWAY VERA CRUZ TO MEXICO.

the north." We arrive at the station of Boca del Monte (mouth of the mountain), about nine o'clock, very cold, but a great breakfast, beginning with soup, going on with many courses, ending with a strange sweetmeat made from honey, and some excellent coffee, makes us forget it, and in half an hour we are pursuing our journey. Boca del Monte is 8,326 feet above the sea, much higher than the valley of Mexico, so that we have to descend on our way there. We have already seen infinitely more than repays us for the long journey we have taken—even the last three hours were more than enough to do that. Were we to turn back now, we should be thankful that we came : shall we be more so as we go on ?

The country is now tame, uninteresting, but for three hours or more we keep Orizaba in sight ; and soon on the left Malintzi, another snow-capped mountain, named by the Indians after Cortez and his Indian mistress, who so much aided his conquest (they called both Malintzi), appears. It is a great, big, beautiful mountain, but not so imposing as its three volcanic neighbours, only because it is not so tall as they are, by some two or three thousand feet, and they are its close neighbours. The immense plain right and left, behind and in front of us as far as the eye can reach, is planted with endless rows of *maguey*, the great Mexican aloe, from which the national drink, *pulque*, is made. Some idea of the magnitude of the pulque trade may be inferred, from the fact, that there is a daily train on the railway between Mexico, Puebla and Vera Cruz, used exclusively in its transport all the year round. But the use of the maguey does not end with pulque; a spirit is distilled from pulque, in taste something between a pleasing liqueur and Scotch whiskey; good vinegar is made from stale pulque; the thick roots of the maguey are used by the Indians in place of soap; brushes are made from the base of its prickly leaves; twine and paper from its fibres; the dry parts of the leaves serve as hones for sharpening razors: textures are made from its filaments, and its sprouts when young, are eaten half roasted. I learn from the Spanish book about the railway that "with justice Father Acosta gave the maguey the name of the 'miraculous plant.'"* At half-past one we stop at Apizaco, but long before reaching it Popocatapetl and Iztaccihuatl have been in view—solemn and grand, their icy peaks glistening in the sun.

---

* I have omitted to notice the town of Huamantla, which we passed about an hour before reaching Apizaco, probably because we were engrossed with Malintzi, which is close to it.

How very big they are!—and yet, perhaps, not *looking* so much so as we expected, for some seven thousand feet of their height is between the plain from which they rise and the sea.

We pass over the plain of Otumba, where Cortes, on his retreat, a few days after his expulsion from Mexico, defeated some two hundred thousand Mexicans, " by his single arm," saving his whole army from destruction ; and for many miles before reaching the little village of San Juan Teotihuacan, we see before us two high mounds of pyramidal form, clothed in green by the trees and shrubs on their sides, one much larger than the other ; we seem close to them as we stop at the station, but they are really some miles off. There is no fit accommodation near, and the only way to visit them will be to come from Mexico, from which they are distant only twenty-eight miles, in the morning, returning in the evening. Indian women and children bring us rough images—heads of terra cotta, and obsidian arrow-heads, turned up by the plough in the neigbourhood of the pyramids, to the train, for sale. We buy a number of them ; they are very rude, but many of the faces have much character and beauty ; strange to say, no two are alike, and we are told no two of them are ever found alike.

There is no doubt of their genuineness.* I am tempted to transcribe for you Prescott's account of these pyramids:

"The monuments of San Juan Teotihuacan are, with the exception of the temple of Cholula, the most ancient remains probably on the Mexican soil. They were found by the Aztecs, according to their traditions, on their entrance into the country, when Teotihuacan (the habitation of the gods), now a paltry village, was a flourishing city, the rival of Tula, the great Toltec capital. The two principal pyramids were dedicated to *Tonatiuh* the Sun and *Meztli* the Moon. The former, which is considerably the larger, is six hundred and eighty-two feet long at the base, and one hundred and eighty feet high, dimensions not inferior to those of some of the kindred monuments of Egypt.† They were divided into four stories, of which three are now discernible, while the vestiges of the intermediate gradations are nearly effaced.

"The interior is composed of clay mixed with pebbles, incrusted on the surface with light porous stone. Over this was a thick coating of stucco, re-

---

* Some of these heads, as we stuck them in the top of a biscuit box, were photographed on our return home, and are published with these letters.

† "The pyramid of Mycerinos is 280 feet only at the base, and 162 feet high; Cheops is 728 feet at the base, and 448 feet high."—*Note from Prescott.*

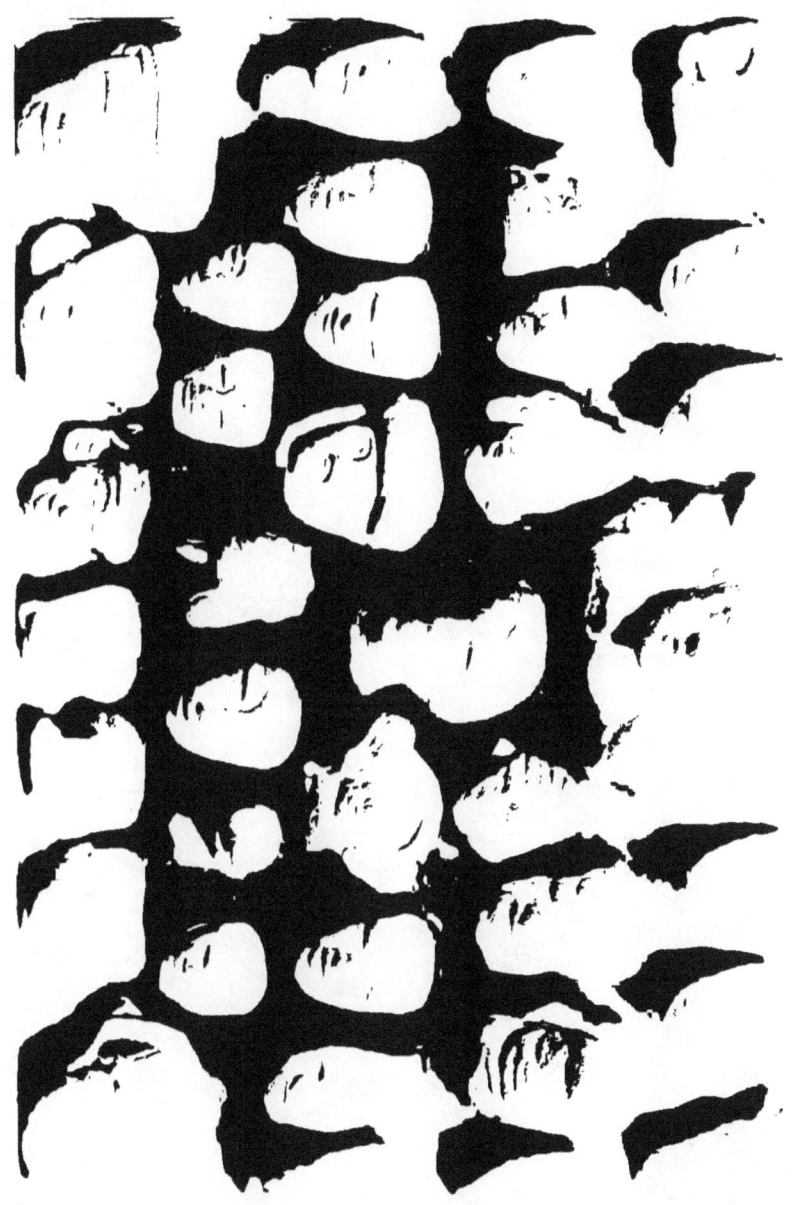

TERRA COTTA HEADS, FROM THE PYRAMIDS OF SAN JUAN TEOTIHUACAN.

sembling in its reddish colour that in the ruins of Palenque. According to tradition, the pyramids are hollow, but hitherto the attempt to discover the cavity in that dedicated to the Sun has been unsuccessful.

"In the other an aperture has been found in the southern side at two-thirds of the elevation.

"It is a narrow gallery, which, after penetrating several yards, terminates in two pits or wells, the largest about fifteen feet deep, the sides faced with unbaked bricks, but to what purpose devoted nothing is left to show.

"It may have been to hold the ashes of some powerful chief, like the solitary apartment in the great Egyptian pyramid. That these monuments were dedicated to religious uses there is no doubt; and it would only be conformable to the practice of antiquity in the Eastern continent, that they should have served for tombs as well as temples.

"Distinct traces of the latter destination are said to be visible on the summit of the smaller pyramid, consisting of the remains of stone walls, shewing a building of considerable size and strength. There are no remains on the top of the pyramid of the Sun.

"The summit of this larger mound is said to have

been crowned by a temple, on which was a colossal statue of its presiding deity, the Sun, made of one entire block of stone, and facing the East.

"On its breast was a plate of burnished gold and silver, on which the first rays of the rising luminary rested.

"It was still standing, according to report, on the invasion of the Spaniards, and was demolished by the indefatigable Bishop Zumarraga, whose hand fell more heavily than that of Time itself on the Aztec monuments. Around the principal pyramids are a great number of smaller ones, rarely exceeding thirty feet in height, which, according to tradition, were dedicated to the stars, and served as sepulchres for the great men of the nation. They are arranged symmetrically in avenues, terminating at the sides of the great pyramids, which face the cardinal points. The plain on which they stand was called *Micoatl*, or 'path of the dead.' But who were the builders? What has become of the races who built them? It is all a mystery, over which Time has thrown an impenetrable veil that no mortal hand may raise. A nation has passed away—powerful, populous, and well advanced in refinement—but it has perished without a name. It has died and made no sign."

Recent excavations show that the country all round these pyramids for a considerable distance is full of small tombs like those about the Egyptian pyramids. It is not an unreasonable belief that this neighbourhood may have been the Memphis of an immense city peopled by this long lost race.

We soon looked down upon "the great valley celebrated in all parts of the world, with its frame work of everlasting mountains, its snow-crowned volcanoes, great lakes, and fertile plains, all surrounding the favoured city of Montezuma," and we strained our eyes to see it and the many towers and spires of the yet distant city; but it was getting darkish; still we might have given the reins to our imaginations, as Madame Calderon (from whom I quote) did, when she first viewed the wonderful panorama before us, and produced something in the way of mental vision; but we didn't, perhaps because we were rather tired with our day's work, and her vision was already before us, and far better than anything we could spirit up. Here it is: "But as we strained our eyes to look into the valley, it all appeared to me more like a vision of the Past than the actual breathing Present. The curtain of Time seemed to roll back, and to discover to us the great panorama that burst upon the eye of Cortés when he first looked down upon the table land—the king-loving, god-fearing conqueror, his loyalty and religion so blended, after the fashion of ancient Spain that it were hard to say which sentiment exercised over him the greater sway. The city of Tenochtitlan, standing in the midst of the five great lakes, upon verdant and flower-covered islands, a western Venice, with thousands of boats gliding swiftly along its streets, long lines of low houses, diversified by the multitudes of pyramidal temples, the Teocali, or houses of God—canoes covering the mirrored lakes —the lofty trees, the flowers, and the profusion of water now wanting to the landscape—the whole fertile valley inclosed by its eternal hills and snow-covered volcanoes—what scenes of wonder and beauty to burst upon the eyes of these wayfaring men ! The beautiful gardens surrounding the city, the profusion of flowers, and fruit, and birds—the wild bronze-coloured Emperor himself advancing, in the midst of his Indian nobility, with rich dress and unshod feet, to receive his unbidden and unwelcome guest—the slaves and the gold, and the rich plumes —all to be laid at the feet of His Most Sacred Majesty—what pictures are called up by the recollection of the simple narrative of Cortés, and how forcibly they return to the mind now, when, after a lapse of three centuries,* we behold for the first time the city of palaces raised upon the ruins of the Indian capital."

In an hour from leaving the pyramids we are close to the waters of Lake Tezcuco; we run round its northern margin, pass the heights of Guadalupe, and soon enter the station. Night has fallen, and we are in the City of Mexico. Leaving our trunks to be looked after by Van W., we seek and find shelter and rest, in what was the palace of the first Emperor, now the Hotel Iturbide: we have large handsome rooms, with brick floors, but nicely carpeted, allotted to us; there is a French restaurant downstairs, where we are to be fed, and the charges there, and for lodging and attendance, all put together, are to come to something short of two dollars and a half, or half a guinea a-day each—more than a dollar and a half a-day less than the like charges at New York and Southern States hotels.

We send back to the station for our trunks, but *not sending the keys,* have to put up with the contents of our bags till the morning. Of course we are very much impressed with being where we are,

---

* Madame Calderon was there in 1839; her husband was the Spanish Minister to Mexico.

and with what I have quoted to you, and try to think of Cortés and the brave adventurers he led, and Montezuma, and all that sort of thing, but truth to tell, we are all of us much absorbed with one idea—as yet only an *idea*—and that is, dinner.

Letter No. 4.

Hotel Iturbide, City of Mexico,
4th March.

WE have been here now more than a week, and, though accustomed to the sights about us, are never tired of viewing and admiring the city and its surroundings. It is not, and you must not expect it to be, quite like Southey's picture as he thus apostrophises it :—

> "Thou art beautiful !
> Queen of the valley ! thou art beautiful !
> Thy walls like silver sparkle in the sun :
> Melodious wave thy groves ; thy garden sweets
> Enrich the pleasant air : upon the lake
> Lie the long shadows of thy towers."

for he was not addressing the Mexico of to-day, and besides, he was writing poetry, and the lake has gone away from the shadows, taking away with it all the beauty its closer proximity contributed ; but Mexico nevertheless *is* beautiful, a gem of a city, with a setting of plain, lakes, suburbs, mountains, that can only be called magnificent.

The lakes are not what they were in the time of Cortés; Lake Chalco is very much smaller, and Lake Tezcuco has not only become much shallower, but its waters have receded two miles and more from the city. As a consequence there is no vestige of the old street canals; they are filled up, and a large fringe of marshy land has taken the place of bright water. The city, too, is much less in area, and infinitely less in population than when its conqueror first came to it; lines and marks are about and around it, plainly indicating the sides of streets and sites of buildings and inclosures of very long ago; and in the business streets many gaps and ruins occur, which we are told are mostly the confiscated properties formerly belonging to the Church.

The present population of the city is something over two hundred thousand; it is well built; the houses large, substantial, and of stone, with flat roofs, are generally built round a patio or yard, entered from the street by a large gateway; the lower story, which is generally used for servants and offices, has its covered gallery all round, and looking out upon this yard, so have the upper stories, looking *down* upon it, and the yard is always open to the sky; the floors and staircases of all the buildings we yet have entered are of marble, stone, or large square

brick. Some of the houses are faced with porcelain, giving them a very pretty effect, as if built in mosaics. There are many fine public buildings and churches, a magnificent cathedral, a fine large plaza, and two beautiful parks, one of them the Alameda.

The suburbs of Chapultepec and Tacubaya are lovely and full of interest, and two of the mountains in the setting I have told you of, Popocatapetl and Iztaccihuatl, are two of the highest, grandest snow-capped volcanoes in the world. I cannot quite make out the form of a reclining woman in the outline of the latter mountain, but the rest of the party can, or think they can. Will you try your imagination with the photograph I send?

By the way, names which but a few days since were puzzles to us, are now as familiar to us as household words; the two big mountains I have just spoken of, and which meet our eyes every day, and a hundred times a day, are (never mind their spelling) "*Po-po-cat-a-pettle,*" "*Iss-tassy-wottle.*" Can anything be more simple and easy? Know, too, that our hotel is called the *Eater-beady.*

The people we meet in streets and public places are motley indeed; all races and all colours seem to be here. The women of the upper classes, the grand ladies of Mexico, so far as we can see and hear, don't walk, but always drive, in public places. The men do, and they appear in the ordinary morning dress suit with the black silk hat worn by English gentlemen; but nine-tenths of those we see are of the industrial classes, and their costumes are new to us, and always more and more taking and picturesque the more we see of them. I must not forget the street cries, or rather the many who cry them: there is the water-carrier, perhaps the strangest in get up and appearance of them all; he has two large globular red porous earthern jars suspended from his shoulders, so large, the wonder is how he can carry them; these he fills at the aqueduct and takes from house to house, slaking the thirst of those who stop him on his way. There is the woman with a brazier of hot charcoal and other apparatus all ready, who wants you to wait while she sits on the curb-stone and cooks you some fish —and there is the fish, sea fish from the gulf, 263 miles off, all ready too, to be cooked—and I see she has a bit simmering in a griddle which has a *very* savoury flavour to the nostrils—wouldn't you like some? And there is another woman with a like brazier and apparatus ready to cook you, now and here, mysterious dishes with many beans and much oil, and garlic and peppers among them. And

PLAZA DE ARMAS, CITY OF MEXICO.
Showing the Cathedral, Sagrario, and National Palace.

there are tortilla and sweet-cake and sweet-meat sellers, and the butcher and the general peddler, and the man selling charcoal strapped to his back like a soldier's knapsack, and a score of others, all strangely picturesque, even if raggedly clothed, and all busily crying their wares in lusty street-cry Spanish. The main streets are generally crowded, and the mules, donkeys, horses, carriages, carts, vehicles of every description, with their drivers and riders, are continual sights to which our eyes open wide. The caballero, as he prances by on his mettled horse always stops us, that we may see more of him and what he wears and carries about him. If his steed were a Rozinante, the rowels of his spurs might almost be made to meet in its middle.

We like to go into the patio of our hotel when the diligences arrive from Toluca and elsewhere. Six mules, and such a jingling and rattling, as they come in! The passengers seem mostly of the caballero class, and are more given to travelling in this fashion than other people.

The street on which the hotel fronts takes us straight to the great square, the plaza de armas, which is about fourteen acres in extent; within it are a park and a lovely garden, the latter planted by the Empress Carlotta. On this plaza front the cathedral, the national palace, the municipal buildings, and a long range of arcaded shops or stores, very solidly built, and of handsome appearance.

The cathedral, like that of Syracuse, is built upon the site of an ancient pagan temple. Where it stands was the great *teocali* (house of God) of the Aztecs. No vestige of this huge pyramid appears, but there is built into the outer wall of the cathedral, low down at its south-east corner, a strange relic of this singular people, indicating their possession of much scientific and astronomical knowledge, called the *Calendar Stone*, which was dug up from the *teocali*, or other adjacent ruins in this great square, in 1790. It is an immense block of black porphyritic rock, rough at its edges, with circles, points, and hieroglyphics deeply carved on it, and by it they had the means of knowing accurately the hours of the day, the times of the solstices and equinoxes, and of the transit of the sun across the zenith of Mexico. The moving of this stone by the Aztecs, who possessed no horses or beasts of burden, is a puzzle to the present day: they brought it from the mountains beyond Lake Chalco, many leagues away, and made it part of the paraphernalia and building of the *teocali*. Its weight before being worked is said to have been nearly fifty

CATHEDRAL, CITY OF MEXICO.

tons; the diameter of the outside circle of the dial is eleven feet eight inches.

I cannot describe a cathedral; but I can say that both outside and inside, especially inside, this one is very beautiful and imposing; it is unlike any I have seen elsewhere. The railings between the choir and the high altar are very fine and costly; they are made of an amalgam of gold, silver, and brass. There is a great deal of finely-carved woodwork representing scriptural scenes, some good paintings, and wherever small columns or pilasters appear about altar or screen, they are of the beautiful Puebla marble or onyx, more like agate than marble. There is a great deal of colour about the church; the service is gorgeous, and the choir and organ both very good. The sacristy is a grand room; the marble and other furnishings of the lavatory for the priests singularly handsome.

Adjoining the cathedral, and connected with it, is the *sagrario* or parish church, Moorish in its architecture, laboriously carved outside, much gilded within; and in and about both a brisk trade of lottery tickets is kept up, their sale bringing in much profit to the church. Both cathedral and sagrario are built on a platform of four or five feet high, made as they are, of the dark porphyritic stone so common here.

But let us go back to the *teocali*, this one being famous in Spanish history. It was of immense size, and upon it, and others like it of larger or smaller dimensions in ancient Anahuac, from twenty to fifty thousand human beings were sacrificed yearly.

The victims were taken to the summit of these pyramids, and placed on the sacrificial stone, their breasts were opened with a heavy sharp knife or hatchet of *aztli* (obsidian), cutting through the ribs as well as flesh, and their hearts torn from them. The hearts quivering with life, were held up towards the sun, which was worshipped throughout Anahuac, and placed at the feet of the God to whom the temple was devoted.

This done, the bodies of the victims were thrown down the pyramid and seized by the multitude to be cooked and form the principal dish at the feasts following the sacrifices; and it would seem they had their Francatellis and Soyers for the purpose. Prescott says of them:—"This was not the coarse repast of famished cannibals, but a banquet teeming with delicious beverages and delicate viands, prepared with art, and attended by both sexes, who conducted themselves with all the decorum of civilized life."

Not far from the cathedral, and fronting on the

great plaza, is an old palace built by Cortés: it is used by the Government for their "Monte Pio" or "Monte de Piedad," a huge pawn-broking establishment. Here you can buy anything, from a brougham to a diamond ring; from a piano to a dressing-case. Money is advanced upon anything and everything, and great bargains are to be picked up occasionally. We were politely shown about the building. As most likely to be interesting, some of the most costly sets of jewels were taken from their strong places and shown to us. Their time for sale had not yet come; some of the sets were very handsome, and had been pledged for many thousand dollars, shown by a ticket annexed to them; they were all old fashioned.

My party one day, without me, went to Guadalupe, and during the journey one of them, L——, had her pocket picked, the only theft we have suffered from as yet. She wore an open pocket, on what Jack would call the starboard quarter of her dress, a pocket borrowed in pattern from the watch pocket of the old four-post bedstead. Into this, when she entered the street car for Guadalupe, was stuffed a pocket-book loaded with seven silver dollars, a pair of gloves, and a handkerchief. Why *will* women wear pockets behind them? They must be as speaking to thieves as the swine to the gipsy in George Barrow's Zincali,—

> "There runs a swine down yonder hill,
>   As fast as e'er he can;
>   And as he runs he *crieth still*,
>   'Come steal me, gipsy man.'"

When L—— left that street car her pocket was empty; surely this is a proof that Mexico possesses a high degree of civilization.

Tempted by what I had heard of Guadalupe, I went there with T—— a few days after this: it is four or five miles off, and is rather a dirty suburb. Street cars are everywhere, and they run to it every half-hour from the plaza; they are first and second class, and drawn by mules on an iron tramway, having much sharper curves than those we see at home. The first-class carriages are clean, comfortable and fast.

Close to the foot of the Guadalupe range, which extends from the city some miles along the valley, is the cathedral, a huge mass of buildings covered with domes and turrets: to its right, as we are facing its front, is a little chapel in which is a chalybeate spring, and two or three hundred yards up the mountain is another and larger chapel: all are dedicated to and built in honour of "our Lady of Guadalupe."

The legend* about her is pretty, and what it tells us came to pass when the conversion of the Aztecs was proceeding but slowly, and when upon this very spot stood an Aztec temple.

It was between the 9th and 12th of December (the day of the month cannot be fixed nearer), in the year 1531, that Juan Diego, a converted Indian, was going up this mountain: passing the spot where the chalybeate spring now is, he heard the sound of sweet music and beheld a rainbow, from which

---

* Under the title of *Santa Maria del Pillar*, our Lady of the Pillar, the blessed Virgin, is styled "Protectress of Saragossa," and is said to have descended from Heaven there, standing on an alabaster pillar, and to have thus appeared to St. James (Santiago) when he was preaching the Gospel in Spain, A.D. 40. The miraculous pillar is preserved in one of the cathedrals at Saragossa. This miracle was so strongly attested, that a Primate of Spain, so late as A.D. 1720, excommunicated those who even questioned it.

Perhaps nearest in resemblance to the legend of Guadalupe is that of the blessed Virgin, under the title of *Santa Maria della Neve*, our Lady of the Snow, to which the magnificent Church of S. M. Maggiore, in Rome, is said to owe its origin. I give it from Mrs. Jamieson's introduction, p. 66:

"A certain Roman patrician, whose name was John (Giovanni Patricio), being childless, prayed of the Virgin to direct him how best to bestow his worldly wealth. She appeared to him in a dream on the night of the fifth of August, 352, and commanded him to build a church in her honour, on a spot where snow would be found the next morning. The same vision having appeared to his wife, and the reigning Pope, Liberius, they repaired in procession the next morning to the summit of Mount Esquiline, where, notwithstanding the heat of the weather, a large patch of ground was miraculously covered with snow, and on it Liberius traced out with his crozier the plan of the church. This story has been often represented in art, and is easily recognised; but it is curious that the two most beautiful pictures consecrated to the honour of the Madonna del Neve are Spanish, and not Roman, and were painted by Murillo about the time that Philip IV. of Spain sent rich offerings to the church of S. M. Maggiore, thus giving a kind of popularity to the legend. They are called in Spanish, S. Maria la Blanca."

suddenly appeared to him a beautiful lady, who told him she was the Blessed Virgin, and that he must go to the bishop and inform him of what he had heard and seen.

This the Indian did, but he made no impression on the mind of the bishop. Again the Virgin appeared to the Indian in the same spot, making the same intimation to him, and telling him to inform the bishop of it, which he does, but the bishop is still incredulous. Three times more the Virgin appeared to Juan Diego, always in the same spot, and at their last meeting she cures his uncle of a serious malady by the waters of the chalybeate spring, which suddenly bursts up from under her feet. She then tells the Indian to go up the mountain nearly to its summit and gather some roses, and that he must take them to the bishop as a proof that the message she now sends by him comes from her; and the message is, that she desires the bishop to "build a church on this mountain, and worship her there as the Virgin of Guadalupe."

Nothing but pines and scrub grew on the mountain, as Juan Diego knew well, for he traversed it daily; but he did as he was told, and found roses blooming in the very spot, where now stands the upper chapel. He hastily plucks and puts them in his *tilma* or blanket, takes them to the bishop, and delivers with them the blessed Virgin's last message. As the bishop takes the flowers from the folds of the blanket, there appears painted on it a beautiful Madonna, the very likeness of the Virgin of Guadalupe. Bishop Zumarraga is astonished, his unbelief is gone, and faith and adoration take its place. Diego is thanked, his uncle called in, and they, with the bishop and his attendants, prostrate themselves before the beautiful image of the Saint. The flowers and the blanket with the miraculous painting on it were transferred by the bishop to the church, in whose custody they yet are, and our Lady of Guadalupe became at once, and has remained ever since, the guardian Saint of Mexico. She was a *native, their own* Saint, and was soon far more in their hearts than "Our Lady of the Remedies," who came from Spain, ever could be;† and

---

† I know of no history from which sprung the name *Our Lady de los Remedios*, nor can I find any in the only authority I possess on the subject—Mrs. Jamieson's charming book, "Legends of the Madonna." I take it, like that of *Santa Maria della Salute*, almost its equivalent, which I *do* find there, to be only "one of the various titles given to the Virgin Mary, and thence to certain effigies and pictures of her, expressive of the wants, the aspirations, the infirmities and sorrows, which are common to poor suffering humanity, or of those divine attributes from which they hoped to find aid and consolation."

The little image of the *Virgen de los Remedios* brought over by Cortés was an object of great reverence with his followers. It was concealed, it is said, on the day following the *noche triste* of his retreat from Mexico; at all events, for some time it disappeared, and was at last found in a maguey plant on the top of a

she made and kept converts by tens of thousands through the length and breadth of the land. And so it came to pass that all these massive and costly churches and buildings were erected; they are all in honour of *Maria Santissima de Guadalupe.*

barren mountain by an Indian. The Spaniards, full of joy and thanksgiving, built a church on the spot, and placed a priest in charge of the "miraculous image." Madame Calderon, writing of it, says:—" Her fame spread abroad, and gifts of immense value were brought to her shrine. A treasurer was appointed to take charge of her jewels, a camarista to superintend her rich wardrobe. No rich dowager died in peace until she had bequeathed to our Lady of los Remedios her largest diamond or richest pearl. In seasons of drought she is brought in from her dwelling in the mountain and carried in procession through the streets. The Viceroy himself, on foot, used to lead the holy train. One of the highest rank drives the chariot in which she is seated. In succession she visits the principal convents, and as she is carried through the cloistered precincts, the nuns are ranged on their knees in humble adoration. Plentiful rains immediately follow her arrival. ———, who accompanied us, has on several occasions filled the office of her coachman, by which means he has seen the interior of most of the convents in Mexico. It is true that there came a time when the famous Curate Hidalgo, the prime mover of the revolution, having taken as his standard, the Virgin of Guadalupe, a rivalry arose between her and the Spanish Virgin: and Hidalgo having been defeated and forced to fly, the image of the Virgen de los Remedios was conducted to Mexico dressed as a General, and invoked as the Patroness of Spain. Later still, the Virgin herself was denounced as a *Gachupina* " (a name given to Europeans in New Spain), " her General's sash boldly torn from her by the valiant General ———, who also signed her passport, with an order for her to leave the Republic. However, she was again restored to her honours, and still retains her treasures, her camarista, and sanctum sanctorum."

Madame Calderon went to see the celebrated image, and thus proceeds:—

" The mountain is barren and lonely, but the view from its summit is beautiful, commanding the whole plain. The church is old and not very remarkable, yet a picturesque object, as it stands in its grey solitariness, with one or two trees beside it, of which one, without leaves, was entirely covered with the most brilliant scarlet flowers.

" Senor ——— having been the Virgin's coachman, the Senora being the daughter of her camarista, and C———n the minister from the land of her pre-

GUADALUPE, MEXICO

(Taken from a balloon).

The upper church, built on the spot where Diego gathered the roses, is reached from the base of the mountain by a handsome stone staircase. Numerous offerings and mementos of the Saint's goodness, curing and saving powers have been placed about it by grateful worshippers.

On the right as you ascend is the mast of a ship with sails set, sculptured in stone, looking very oddly

---

dilection, we were not astonished at the distinguished reception which we met with from the reverend padre, the guardian of the mountain.

"The church within is handsome, and above the altar is a copy of the original Virgin. After we had remained there a little while we were admitted into the sanctum, where the identical Virgin of Cortés, with a large silver maguey, occupies her splendid shrine. The priest retired and put on his robes, and then returning, and all kneeling before the altar, he recited the *credo*. This over, he mounted the steps, and, opening the shrine where the Virgin was encased, knelt down and removed her in his arms. He then presented her to each of us in succession, every one kissing the hem of her satin robe.

"The image is a wooden doll, about a foot high, holding in its arms an infant Jesus, both faces evidently carved with a rude pen-knife: two holes for the eyes and another for the mouth. This doll was dressed in blue satin and pearls, with a crown upon her head, and a quantity of hair fastened on to the crown: no Indian idol could be much uglier. As she has been a good deal scratched and destroyed in the lapse of ages, C——n observed, that he was astonished they had not tried to restore her a little. To this the padre replied, that the attempt had been made by several artists, each one of whom had sickened and died. He also mentioned as one of her miracles that, living on a solitary mountain, she had never been robbed; but I fear the good padre is somewhat *oblivious*, as this sacrilege has happened more than once. On one occasion a crowd of *léperos* being collected, and the image carried round to be kissed, one of them, affecting intense devotion, bit off the large pearl that adorned her dress in front, and before the theft was discovered he had mingled with the crowd and escaped. When reminded of the circumstance, the padre said it was true, but that the thief was a *Frenchman*."

Can any parallel to this story of setting off Imperial against Colonial Saint, the one to check, the other to aid rebellion, be found in the history of the war between England and her North American colonies?

out of place. This was erected by a gentleman who was shipwrecked at Vera Cruz, and whose life was saved, as he devoutly believed, by the interference of the Virgin of Guadalupe. We entered the cathedral, passing through a crowd of beggars at its door. It is very fine in many respects, and is gorgeous with gilt and silver and ornament. There is some beautiful wood carving, and a double railing from choir to altar is of solid silver. I am afraid to say how long or high, or thick or valuable it is, lest you might think I exaggerated. Organ and choir are magnificent; music, and the grandest of all, sacred music, is at home in Mexico.

What most obtained our attention though, was the great earnestness and devotion of the hundreds who were joining in the service; all alike seemed engrossed in most humble earnest prayer.

I wonder if it was wicked in me to think that they were not praying to the Almighty—the King of Kings and Lord of Lords—but to " our Lady of Guadalupe."

There is a School of Art in Mexico which possesses some fine paintings, among them some genuine Murillos; there is also a School of mines and a museum. In the latter we could find nothing open to the public save two or three rooms

devoted to natural history; but looking about the offices of the building, I met a gentleman who kindly unlocked the rooms, in which, besides the library, were the antiquities we were so desirous to see. In the library were Lord Kingsborough's book and Humboldt's "Flora of Mexico." Among the antiquities, quaint old Aztec things, idols, jars, vases, rude musical instruments, two or three heavy sacrificial yokes of stone, mirrors of obsidian, in which Aztec ladies performed their toilette; also, among a thousand other strange things, were the victorious banner of Cortés, with a lovely Madonna face pictured on it, and the feather shield of Montezuma. Everything was higgledy piggledy about the rooms; no order or arrangement. In the court below was an immense sacrificial stone strangely sculptured, a hollow in its top for the head, and channels for the blood of the victim; and there, too, was a huge hideous stone idol of their god of war, at whose feet the victim's heart was offered. Both came from the *teocali*, which stood where the cathedral now is.

The face of this idol is heavy and stolid: it is, I should say, not the war-god of the Aztecs seen by Cortés in its temple, on the top of this *teocali*, by permission of Montezuma; the idol he saw was horrible to look at, and had a great deal of gold and many precious stones and pearls inlaid in and about it. Prescott describes it closely, and adds:

"The most conspicuous ornament was a chain of gold and silver hearts alternate, suspended round his neck, emblematical of the sacrifice in which he most delighted. A more unequivocal evidence of this was afforded by three human hearts smoking, and almost palpitating, as if recently torn from the victims, and now lying on the altar before him."

Of the temple or chapel it was in, and of another, he says:

"The walls were stained with human gore. 'The stench was more intolerable,' exclaims Diaz, 'than that of the slaughter-houses in Castile!'"

I cannot leave these two horrid stones without mention of the pyramid of skulls of the victims found in this *teocali*, counted by one of the soldiers at one hundred and thirty-six thousand! "Belief," says Prescott, "might well be staggered, did not the old world present a worthy counterpart in the pyramid of Golgothas, which commemorated the triumphs of Tamerlane."

The old market is always interesting to visit, for you see there still much that was so well described by the Spaniards more than three hundred years ago, with the very same costumes and people: it is

THE PASEO, CITY OF MEXICO.

Equestrian Statue of Charles V., Chapultapec, the Aqueduct, Paseo a T...

close to the plaza and the palace, and at the end of the canal which brings it vegetables, fruit—a hundred things. The fruits are delicious. We have eaten and enjoyed the mango, and have many different rich fruits in abundance daily; one is just like Charlotte Russe, another like butter!

Some of the streets are exceptionally fine; that of San Francisco, on which our hotel fronts, is one of the best. It runs easterly by many names to the plaza, and westerly by many other names past the beautiful alameda or park, wherein, by the way, you are not safe from robbery after dusk. The railway history book says: "The Alameda had an opening near the Convent of San Diego, called the 'Quemadero,' from the stone brazier for burning victims of the Inquisition. The Viceroy, Marquis de Croix, in 1766, ordered it to be destroyed, and gave the alameda the space it now possesses." Beyond this the street goes into the *paseo*, the great drive, rotten-row and promenade of all Mexico. There you will see the caballero on his beautiful horse, in all his pride and grandeur : such a hat! made of fine light-coloured felt, wide as an umbrella, laced with gold or silver cord, and costing as much, perhaps, as thirty English hats : his dress too elaborate for my description, and his spurs looking as if made for slaughter, not for speeding. There are carriages and vehicles handsome and humble, horsemen and mule-men of every sort and description: among the former, English broughams and other carriages of faultless make, colour, and finish, the horses and harness perfect. You see ladies beautifully dressed, and you see the dress and get up, by thousands, of everybody in the country, high and low, and of very many who come from other lands. The *paseo* in the afternoon is a sight to see again and again. For a certain length, about three miles, it is guarded by cavalry on either side, doing duty as mounted police: beyond, some two miles or so, is Chapultepec, which was the home of Montezuma and his race; and beyond that again, some two miles, is Tacubaya, a large village with beautiful parks, villas and gardens, where the rich of Mexico love to dwell and to visit.

We have been to Chapultepec again and again: it is surrounded by a high fence: entering by a large gate close to the high road, we are at once in its grounds, and among huge venerable trees, one of which, a cyprus, *fifty feet in circumference*, is called "Montezuma's tree," from his being much accustomed to sit under it. Not far from this tree rises abruptly the high hill or mass of rock

CHAPULTEPEC, MEXICO.

on which is the picturesque building called the castle of Chapultepec, built by the Viceroy Galvez in the seventeenth century. We found its topmost tower being fitted up for the convenience of some astronomers who were shortly to be in Mexico to watch the transit of Venus. The rooms are, some of them, fine, but everywhere there is a look of desertion—of the empty house. It is used but now and then, and only for State occasions, and though Maximilian delighted in it, there is little or nothing within its walls that we are permitted to see to remind us that he was ever here.

I cannot properly describe the view from the castle. It is beyond me. Immediately below it, are its own beautiful grounds; beyond, the villas, churches, groves, parks, and gardens of Tacubaya. Again, beyond them, Popocatapetl and Iztaccihuatl. To the left, and in front, are the distant city and valley, with vistas of the lakes, intensely brilliant in blue : more to the left are the sierra of Guadalupe; and everywhere, behind and around, and framing the panorama, are mountains, rich in colour and bold and beautiful in outline. Is there any such spot for royal residence in the world ? Descending, we go out at the gate by which we entered, noticing now, if we have not before, the pool and rills known as Montezuma's bath, near to which, taking the waters of Chapultepec to the city, begins the famous San Cosme aqueduct, a picturesque old stone structure, supported by arches.

One of the roads leading to the city, passing that huge amphitheatre, the *plaza de toros*, the now unused bull-fight building, and entering the *paseo* at its upper end, is known as the "Empress's Drive." It was made by Maximilian at her desire.

Again we came out in this direction, going to Tlanetantla, some fourteen miles or more from Chapultepec, so that we have seen the country all round it. To get to Tlanetantla we took the street cars from the plaza for some four or five miles, and then a locomotive displaced the mules and took us on; but there is nothing to see at Tlanetantla, except that you get nearer the base of the mountains surrounding the valley.

You will gather some idea of what Chapultepec and the views from it are by the photographs; for what it was in the time of Montezuma I must refer you to your books.

There is a foundry and manufactory for brass cannon and other arms at Molino del Rey, close by Chapultepec, and at Tacubaya is the military college, neither of which we have visited yet.

We have all of us been a little distressed by the rarified atmosphere, as most strangers are—I, more so than the others. During the first few nights of our coming I used to wake up gasping, and rush to and open the window to breathe the better, returning to bed chilled and cold with the night air. Getting up-stairs, too, was trying, and is yet to us all.

Not knowing what this meant, I consulted Dr. S——, the United States Consul-General, who kindly came to see me. His diagnosis was very prompt. "Do you know," he asked, "that you are thirty-seven times higher up in the air than the top of the steeple of Trinity Church in Broadway, New York?" I found that changing my room from a northern to a southern aspect completely removed this trouble.

For some days before reaching Vera Cruz, acting from what I had read, and on the advice of our medical attendant, I had given my party daily doses of quinine, as a preventive against fever, which Dr. S—— says is quite right; but he adds, "continue it here, for there is a great deal of malaria from bad drainage and the subsidence of the lakes." Puebla he speaks very approvingly of.

The days are very hot in the sun, which is vertical, but there is always a cool, sometimes a cold, breeze and air coming from the mountain tops and sides. Half an hour or so before the sun sets comes a chilliness that tells us his warmth is passing away, and how much more pleasant this great altitude is with it than without it.

A fire in the evening would be very nice to have, for we are, so to speak, in a well—a deep cellar, walled up with high mountains; but no fire can be had: there is no fire-place.

England has no representative in Mexico, and the United States minister is absent; but Mrs. F—— shows us much hospitality and kindness, enables us to see something of the English-speaking society, and is especially good to T——, who, but for this, would know much less of Mexican manners, customs, and shops.

My letter is more than long enough. Addio!

Letter No. 5.

HOTEL ITURBIDE, CITY OF MEXICO,
7th March.

ON Tuesday last we had an expedition on the canal, a party from the American Consulate accompanying us. Driving up the paseo de la Viga, and passing a square wherein stood a bust of Guatemozin (there is none of Montezuma anywhere), we reached a bridge crossing the canal which runs into, or rather out of Lake Chalco, and getting into a large flat bottomed boat, with comfortable seats and an awning, were quietly poled along by a couple of Indians for some miles, to a village called Ixtacalco, where was a very old church built by Cortés.

There had been within the city carnival making to some extent, yet but little, owing to the recent death of Pio Nono, for whose memory the inhabitants have a great and sincere respect, and many windows were draped in mourning in consequence. But at Ixtacalco was a small party of mummers who rather persecuted us with absurd music and gesture, following us some little distance, perhaps only the way they were going, along the bank of the canal. We went all about and on top of the old church, which was dirty and dilapidated, and looked as if not much prayed in or cared for. This appears to be the condition of numbers of churches all over the country; its cause, either a decrease in religious feeling, or the stripping of the church by the government, of so much of its property and revenues; however this may be, it is apparent that the masses of the Mexican people, with or without those above them, and however tolerant their government may be, are disinclined to permit any church other than their own to live and flourish among them.

We went into the little churchyard. About the graves were heaps of bleached skulls and bones—a common, but very unpleasing spectacle in Mexican churchyards. In coming and returning we passed many large boats laden with country produce, going to the market, and, I must not forget to say, many island, but not *floating*, gardens: the days of the latter are past, the former flourish and are made thus:—A piece of ground being selected along the back of the canal, a ditch is dug at its rear and parallel with the canal, other ditches are dug from the canal to this, at right angles to it across the piece of ground, which is thus made into many islands, easily irrigated from the ditches surrounding them, and accessible by them from the canal.

We get glimpses both of Lake Chalco and Lake Tezcuco during the day. The latter is ten miles long, six wide—looking at it, I should have thought it much more. A day or two since we heard there was a steamer running on it, and we at once had the desire to go all over the lake in that steamer, and see all its coast and explore its beautiful mountain setting. We thought of newspapers, handbills, placards, to find that steamer; but they don't do that sort of thing in Mexico; you must find out all things as you best can; the manager of the hotel couldn't tell us, but he said we had better get a carriage and drive to two or three places he named, and we might learn all we wanted.

We did as we were told, and after much driving and questioning, to our great disappointment, we at last got this information:—1. The lake was at this season too shallow for the steamer. 2. The steamer had burst her boiler!

We have visited the palace, a fine building extending along the east side of the plaza, and have had the honour of an interview with President Diaz.

A party from the United States Consulate accompanied us, and so our admission was a matter of no difficulty. The courts and lobbies about the ground floor are filled with soldiers. Soon an old Colonel, on the staff of the President takes charge of us and shows us what is to be seen. Mr. C——, a talented member of the New York Press, is with the Consulate party, and he interprets.

The hall of the ambassadors is the chief, and a magnificent room. Its length is about a hundred and eighty feet, its width hardly sufficient for its length. Portraits of the leading Generals and Presidents hang on its walls, with some other paintings, among them one of the *noche triste*, depicting the terrible attack upon Cortés and his band on the causeways during the night of their retreat.

The picture is by a native artist, is large and very elaborate, requiring much time to master its details; but it seemed to me to want light, without which no picture, especially those containing many figures, can be a success: you looked through an atmosphere of darkness at large masses of figures fighting, struggling, and upon no figure or group was the flame of torch or other light brought to bear by the artist as it seemed to me it should have been.

Asked if we should like to see the President, we

GENERAL PORFIRIO DIAZ,
President of the Republic of Mexico.

said, certainly we *should*, but we could not think of intruding upon his time.

We were told however, that the President would see us, and we were taken from the hall of Ambassadors to a smaller room and seated. Soon an aid-de-camp passes us with a paper, as if on business, but evidently to see what manner of people we were. The President* shortly enters—he is of middle height, slight rather than stout, graceful, genial in manner, a pure Indian, and is dressed in ordinary morning costume ; we rise and are presented by Mr. C——, who tells the President in Spanish shortly, who each of us is ; we are all made to sit again, and the President has some words of conversation for us all, the right word always in the right place ; there was that well-bred ease and repose about his manner which is so rarely met with—how did he acquire it or is it simply Aztec high breeding ? The son of an

---

* Prince Salm-Salm in his "last days of the Emperor Maximilian." London, Richard Bentley, 1868, thus sketches the history of General Porfirio Diaz :— "He commanded one of the large military divisions in which the country was divided, and that particularly which contained his home. He had distinguished himself in the battle of Santa Lorette, where he had a higher command. When Puebla was taken later, he fell into the hands of the French, but succeeded in escaping on his way to Vera Cruz. Later he organized a corps, but which was dispersed by the Austrians, who again made him a prisoner, and brought him to Puebla where he remained several months, until he found another opportunity of escaping. On his way he collected seven men with whom he went to his home, where this modest commencement of an army increased in the course of the year to twelve thousand men, with whom he besieged and took Mexico."

English peer was with us, and to him were addressed a few graceful words having allusion to his father. To my reminder that Halifax was as near to Mexico as New York on the Atlantic, and that Vancouver was not much further than San Francisco on the Pacific, and that Canada desired to have a large interchange of products with Mexico, the President said, "he knew the position and advantages of the ports I had mentioned; the policy of his government was to foster commerce with all countries, and already a trade had commenced with Canada."

Rising, he gave his arm to T——, and we all followed. He showed us what had been the bed-room and boudoir of the Empress Carlotta; her dressing-room beyond them, he said was occupied. Showing us a beautiful cabinet made of many woods of the country covered in part with its marble, he said it was intended to go to the Centennial Exhibition, but was not completed in time. We saw a few vases and other things bearing the cipher of Maximilian.

Taking leave of us at a side door leading down to the gardens of the palace, he placed us again in charge of our former escort the colonel, who took us over them and then to the armoury.

In the gardens the only thing worthy of note we saw was the hand tree, "*el arbol de las manitas,*" probably the same tree Madame Calderon speaks of; it was covered with bright scarlet flowers in the form of a hand, with five fingers and a thumb.

The gardener gave us a number of them, and we tried to preserve some but without success. This tree is very rare, there being only one or two others in the country.

We next visit the armoury. As we enter we see suspended high on the bare wall opposite to us, and far apart, two small stands of arms. They are those with which the two Emperors were shot to death.

Wondering whose savage taste directed this exhibition, I said to the colonel: "I suppose these are here as a sort of proclamation that you want no more Emperors?" He laughed loudly, and nodded in reply.

In the night I thought of these stands of arms, and how one of them had taken the life of the Emperor Maximilian, the reason of the Empress, and how infinitely sadder and more awful is her fate than was his.*

---

* Prince Salm Salm, who was the Emperor's "first aide-de-camp and Chief of the Household" says, in his book already referred to, that the general belief was, that if the Emperor had fallen into the hands of Porfirio Diaz instead of those of Escobedo, he would not have been shot. But who can say? From the stand point of the Juarez Government what were they to do otherwise? The Emperor had shot their generals, taken in arms against his government; should they not shoot *him*, taken in arms against *theirs?* Their first Emperor

F

The foot of Popocatapetl is within twelve or fifteen miles of us, and you may expect me to tell you I have stood on its topmost peak, but I must disappoint you. When a mountain is accessible by rail, as are Rigi and Mount Washington, or even without rail if it be no higher than Helvellyn or Vesuvius, I approve of getting to the top of it; but where you have to toil, labour and struggle, to perspire and freeze, to cut notches for your feet in getting up a sloping wall of ice, to be tied to a

---

had pledged himself never to leave Europe or trouble them again; but he had broken his word; and what assurance had they that their second would not break his? If he were dead, the government would be assured; if he lived, there would be a mine under it ready to explode, at any moment. Add to this, the feeling of rancour and hot blood—and that *Mexican blood*—against the Imperialists, and the result was inevitable.

The following letter extracted from Prince Salm-Salm's book, speaks volumes as to the character of the unfortunate Emperor. He was to be shot on the 19th of June; all hope of escape had been abandoned; on the 18th he writes the letter, dating it the following day, to be delivered then:—

"Queretraro, June 19th, 1867.

"M. Benito Juarez.— On the point of suffering death, because I desired to try whether new institutions would enable me to put an end to the bloody war which for so many years has been causing ruin to this unhappy country, I will yield up my life with satisfaction, if this sacrifice can contribute to the welfare of my adopted country.

"Being fully convinced that nothing durable can be produced on a soil soaked in blood, and moved by violent agitation, I implore you, in the most solemn manner, and with that sincerity which is peculiar to moments like those in which I find myself, that my blood may be the last that may be spilled, and that the same perseverance which I appreciated when in the midst of prosperity, and with which you defended the cause that conquers now, might be applied to the most noble end to reconcile all the hearts, and to rebuild on a durable, firm foundation, the peace and order of this unhappy country.

"(Signed)   Maximilian."

THE VOLCANO OF POPOCATAPETL.
17,783 feet high.
(From a photo. by Kilburn Brothers.)

rope with other foolish people tied to it above, others below you, a precipice behind and on either side of you, to be pulled up and down slopes and precipices by the rope when there is no foot-hold—in a word to be in a state of dirt, heat, cold, hunger, thirst, fatigue, risk, from base to summit, and from summit to base, I can only say, with the certainty of being despised by the members of the Alpine Club, and all people like them—*le jeu n'en vaut pas la chandelle,* and I will stay humbly below. What a state one's lungs and brain would be in at the top of this mountain, which is 1,945 feet higher than Mont Blanc! But people *do* ascend it.* We met a lady at the United States Consulate, Miss R——, who had been up. She was young and strong, but seemed to speak of it with a sort of shiver. One gentleman of her party, which was, fortunately for him, numerous and well-appointed became fright-

* The first ascent and descent into the crater was made under the orders of Cortés, by Francisco Montano, one of his officers, with a party of four. "They climbed to the very edge of the crater, which presented an irregular ellipse at its mouth, more than a league in circumference. Its depth might be from 800 to 1,000 feet. A lurid flame burned gloomily at the bottom, sending up a sulphureous steam, which, evolving as it rose, was precipitated on the ridge of the cavity. The party cast lots, and it fell on Montano himself to descend in a basket into this hideous abyss, into which he was lowered by his companions to the depth of 700 feet! This was repeated several times, till the adventurous cavalier had collected a sufficient quantity of sulphur for the wants of the army."—PRESCOTT.

fully ill, and, in a state of insensibility was carried and lowered, and lowered and carried, and in that state brought down; he did not recover for some weeks.

The ascent is made from Amcca-Meca: in twelve hours you get to a ranch where you sleep; at something short of 13,000 feet above the sea all vegetation ceases, and nearly to this, the mountain is covered thickly with forest; above, it is strewed with pumice, sand and ashes from the crater, and covered with snow and ice. The sand affords a very dangerous footing, large fields of it often sliding downwards. The crater is more than three miles in diameter and more than a thousand feet deep; it has been descended to the depth of 700 feet. There is a hut above the ranch, and the ascent from this is more laborious troublesome and dangerous than the rest. The cold is extreme. There has been no active eruption since 1540, but the mountain still smokes, and Humboldt saw ashes being emitted from it when he ascended it.

I could find no one who had ascended or heard of any one who had ascended Iztaccihuatl: being some 2,000 feet lower than her husband and neighbour, she does not receive the attention he does.

The sierra of Ahualco, a curtain-like ridge

stretching north and south, connects the two volcanoes; at the pass of Ahualco where Cortés descended to the table-land and into the valley of Mexico, the height is but about 10,000 feet above the sea.

I have spoken of the confiscation of the property of the Church: with it came freedom of opinion in religion and religious belief and that sweeping change which removed all the direct and acknowledged influence and control of Church over State introduced by the Spaniards, which was almost supreme, and which so long survived the independence of the country. Comonfort and Juarez were the final movers in this revolution, and what the former left undone the latter accomplished; doubtless the fall of Maximilian was the beginning of the end, if the end has yet come.

Not only has church property been confiscated, including that in convents and monasteries, but those institutions have been abolished and are forbidden, and a sponge has been passed through manifold debts secured to the Church all the country over by mortgage. Schools were established free of church control; religious processions were prohibited; churches and convent buildings were soon for sale everywhere, and the latter are now often occupied as hotels, or in some other way foreign to their original purpose.

But a few years since and the burial service of the Protestant Church could not be read over their dead; and woe to that man who, while the *Host* was being carried past, did not throw himself on his knees before it!

The change has been great indeed, and extraordinary in this, that the bulk of the population, it might be said nearly all who possessed any religion, were and are still Roman Catholics.

And so it is not surprising although all this has come to pass, and although the priest is never seen in the streets or public places in cassock or robe, that the Church has still great influence in the country.

The first blow practically struck at church property fell within a hundred yards of this hotel. The street on which it fronts runs now from the plaza past the alameda without interruption, and is one of the principal thoroughfares of Mexico; but, in the time of Comonfort and before, it did not; the grand church and convent of San Francisco, or rather the masses of building connected with them, blocked the way. Comonfort determined the street should be continued, used the power of his government for the purpose and put down with a strong hand the opposition offered by the Church. This portion of the street is now called the street of the Independence. Concurrently with this came the end of that cruel and persecuting intolerance of all other churches and forms of religion but their own; and now, and for some years past men, individually and collectively, may *openly*, lawfully worship their Maker according to their own consciences.

The law and the government permit this; but the people in many parts of the country are disinclined to do so, and have again and again shown how much the old feeling prevails among them by riot and violence.

This new toleration brought to the country many Protestant missionaries from the United States, foremost among them the Reverend Dr. Riley of the Episcopal Church, whom I have the good fortune to know. With him worked in common other missionaries from the Methodists, Baptists, and Presbyterians, and, according to their published accounts, with much success.

Dr. Riley has obtained a church for his congregation; the Reverend Dr. Butler, of the Methodists, another for his—both solid handsome stone structures; and I believe churches are to be had at a very reasonable price all over the country.

Of late, I understand each of these Protestant denominations has thought it best to do its own work, and get its aid separately.

We hoped to meet Dr. Riley here, but we shall be disappointed, as he is detained in New York longer than he expected.

I wish I could tell you what he has done and is likely to do, as I know it would much interest you. His heart is in his work, and he is energetic and sanguine, but he and others like him are often in danger of their lives, and already two or more lives of missionaries have been taken.

There is a soreness among the Mexicans because the United States Government have not yet recognised that of President Diaz. Speaking to an Englishman about it, he said the delay was simply that the United States might get a better tariff for their goods—its professed doubts about the stability of the Diaz Government not existing at all. I have seen Jonathan's " notions " even in Malta and Sicily; his rifles and bayonets in the hands of the soldiers of the Khedive. (What was Birmingham about?) He is always on the alert—always trying to get his products into other countries cheaply, or for nothing if he can, but he won't let other people's come into his on the same terms. Is

NATIVE SILVERSMITHS.

he right or not? I have immense respect, for his judgment on such a question, I must confess.

I feel, with all my letter writing how very little idea of the country, the city, or the people, I have conveyed to you; but to understand, you must see. I have not mentioned a hundredth part of what we see and hear. I have not told you of the native silversmiths and their street, (their work is far more solid than that of the Genoese, and fully as beautiful), the flower-girls, and the scores of other street and country people we see continually, and I have said no word about the strange plump black pigs that turn up in unexpected places by units and tens; but they are only *pig-skins* full of *pulque;* nor have I told you how new, striking, and attractive to the eye the dress and person of every individual and group we meet is; but the photographs will help me, and I shall finish this letter by quoting some words from Madame Calderon de la Barca's book about Mexico.

"There is not one human being or passing object to be seen that is not in itself a picture, or which would not form a good subject for the pencil. The Indian women with their plaited hair and little children slung to their backs, their large straw hats and petticoats of two colours, the long strings of carriers with their loaded mules and swarthy wild looking faces—the chance horseman who passes with his scrape of many colours, his high ornamental saddle, Mexican hat, silver stirrups and leathern boots, all is picturesque. Salvator Rosa and Hogarth might have travelled here to advantage, hand in hand."

There is an excellent school system working now in cities and towns, and we intended to visit some of them here, but our time is too short. For the same reason we have to omit the public cemetery, where lie many of Mexico's great men (very few of whom by the way died in their beds), also, the American and English cemeteries and the gardens of Tivoli and many other places.

T—— has given me a scrap of her writing for you, to add to my letter, and here it is :—

"We are much disappointed in the *gala* dress of the peasantry, having seen nothing of the fine lace, bright coloured satins or gold and silver embroidery, we were led to expect. The diamond rings and other jewels we were to see too must be now all in the *monte pio*.

"The red and black striped petticoat is to be seen with an over dress of Manchester print, which last is more common in Mexico now perhaps than formerly.

"The usual dress is a skirt of a yellowish brown stuff with an over dress of bright print; a print handkerchief arranged with some grace over the head, and a reboso, an indispensable adjunct to the dress of a Mexican woman.

"The flower sellers are the most picturesque in appearance; they wear a white boddice with a bright flowing skirt, and carry a large basket of flowers on the head, another on the right arm, the left hand full of bouquets; this, with the reboso thrown over the left shoulder makes up a very graceful picture, especially if the woman happens to be pretty.

"While on the subject of dress you may be interested to hear of the luxurious manner in which a Mexican lady does her shopping. She never thinks of leaving her carriage, but lets the shopmen rush out to her—no, no one rushes in Mexico,—they walk out to her deliberately, bringing silks, laces, lawns, every thing that she can possibly want. Perhaps one reason, or *the* reason that she does not leave her carriage is, that she has *no shoes or stockings* on, for Mexican ladies when driving rarely wear them, though they are most elaborately dressed otherwise. They are usually without a bonnet, but always with a fan, *à l'Espaynol:* they lean back in their carriages with a languid air, not even exerting themselves to bow to their friends, but merely making a motion with the hand which was not inaptly described to us as 'twirling their fingers.' A good deal of coquetry is often practised in this way, as much depends on the manner in which the twirling is done. A pretty hand, flashing diamond rings (for gloves are left at home with the shoes and stockings), sparkling eyes, half concealed by the fan, caballeros passing and repassing that the twirling may be repeated, prove that the Mexican ladies are not less accomplished coquettes than their American or European sisters."

I have omitted to tell you that opals are plentiful here and very cheap; the best we have seen for sale have been those brought to the hotel; many of them are large, but none are extraordinary otherwise.

We are very comfortable here and shall leave the Iturbide with regret; its restaurant and its cookery are excellent; the *chef*, a Frenchman, always honours us by bringing in what he thinks the best dish himself, and everybody in the house is attentive and obliging.

To-morrow, we leave for Puebla.

Letter No. 6.

HOTEL VERA CRUSANO, VERA CRUZ,
13th March.

" These mountains piercing to the sky
With their eternal cones of ice,
Change not, but still remain as ever,
Unwasting, deathless and sublime."
— *Albert Pike*.

" There is a wakening on the mighty hills,
A kindling with the spirit of the morn !
Bright gleams are scattered from the thousand rills,
And a soft, visionary hue is born."
—*Mrs. Hemans*.

Y last letter was finished as we were about to leave the City of Mexico. The diary will tell you what we have done and seen since.

8th March.

We leave the Iturbide this morning at six o'clock, driving to the station in the dark. We had seen the two great volcanoes daily in all their changes of light, shade and colour, but never as we were about to see them.

As the train runs along between the sierra of

Guadalupe and the shore of Lake Tezcuco, the sun rises and lights up their snowy heads and the mountain peaks about with a rosy tinge which makes the lake purple, and the whole valley, as far as the eye can reach a scene never to be forgotten.

How superb it all was, and what a delightful last impression of our visit it has become!

At Apizaco, an official of the railway, an Englishman finds us out and offers me, as a fellow-countryman, his private rooms for the toilet of my party after their very dusty journey. No attention could have been more thoughtful or half so welcome, and it is gratefully accepted. In one of this gentleman's rooms was a fire-place, the only one we have met with in the country.

The restaurant and its coffee and Bordeaux wine are excellent, but the accommodation otherwise is *nil*.

From Apizaco, as the translation of the Spanish railway book says, "the most admirable perspectives are enjoyed, developing the cordilleras; to the south-east the Malintzi, and, far away in the distance, the Cofre de Perote, Orizaba and the Sierra Negra; to the north, the mountains of Tlaxco, and to the south-west Iztaccihuatl and Popocatapetl."

While in Mexico we were on the other side of the two latter, and now have seen well round them.

We arrive at Puebla at half-past three, getting on the way a good look at the plain and heights of Tlascala, whose people gave Cortés at first so much hindrance and trouble—at last, much great help—in his subjugation of Mexico.

For the last hour of our journey a "norther" was blowing and clouds of sand were all about us. Driving to the hotel de diligentias, which is a very large house built in the usual way round a large square court, and ascending a great stone staircase we get to the second story, whose rooms open upon a wide arched cloister-looking stone gallery, open outside its arches to the sky above, and to the court below; around this gallery are placed tropical plants and flowers, and there is an aviary full of strange birds of brilliant plumage, who fill the air with song that is chirruppy and cheerful, if not musical. Three large rooms are assigned to us opening upon this gallery; the restaurant is good, and we think with reason we are well put up; the prices are less than at the Iturbide.

Like all others here, the building is of stone; it was formerly a theological college, more lately a convent; its iron gateway leading to our gallery has yet over it the initials I. H. S.—strange to meet in an hotel, but out of place no where.

Puebla is well built, its streets are wide, its churches numerous, many of them grand and imposing; it has its plaza and alameda, and there is an air of brightness and order everywhere.

The principal churches are the cathedral, which is smaller than that of Mexico, but finer, the Campăna or Jesuits' Church, and that of San Francisco.

The cathedral occupies one side of the plaza, and like that of Mexico, stands on an immense stone platform, raised four or five feet from the plaza; it is built of a very dark porphyritic stone with massive buttresses and lofty towers; within the effect is very imposing; huge columns eighty or ninety feet high support a well-lighted and graceful roof.

Like the other two churches, it is rich in gilding, carvings, inlaid wood-work, beautiful marble, fine paintings.

Nowhere we think have we seen anything to equal, certainly we have not to excel, the grandeur and beauty of its interior.

Its chapter room is hung with tapestries worked by the ladies of the court of one of the Spanish kings who presented them to the cathedral. In the sacristy are some fine old paintings; the lavatory for the priests, with its beautiful marble is finer than that in the cathedral of Mexico : and we shall none of us forget the full sweet rich tone of its organ and bells.

But I have not told you that Puebla is a city of the angels, its name in full being "Puebla de los Angelos." Cholula, some eight or more miles off, was, when Cortés came, and nobody knows how long before, the paganest, of all pagan towns in ancient Anahuac ; there, was among any number of others, its biggest *teocali*, the now known all the world over pyramid, dedicated to their good deity Quetzalcoatl who founded the place, and introduced and fostered there everything that was clever and useful and pure and good. This god as you know had long gone off on some foreign tour, and was expected back about the time of the arrival of Cortés, fortunately for the latter as it turned out ; but all this time, rites and ceremonies, sacrifices to the number of fifteen or twenty thousand human beings yearly were continually going on at Cholula, in honour of the absent Quetzalcoatl, and every body who had any religion at all went there to participate. In a word, it was the Mecca of the ancient Mexicans. It was but natural that the Spaniards should desire to found close to such a place, a large Christian city. In this

G

desire Puebla had its origin, and it is perhaps not to be wondered at, that many wished and thought, and then said, and then believed, that "Angels aided the building of the new city by night, and sang songs over its builders by day."

But for all this a royal ordinance from Spain was required and obtained for its foundation in the year 1530; from the same authority came letters patent in 1571 establishing there the Inquisition. The buildings formerly used by this institution are very large, substantial and costly. Puebla has always possessed a population strongest of all in Mexico in its adherence to the church introduced by the Spaniards, and there, are yet to be found with no break in their ranks, its most pious and loyal followers.

It is a city fair to see, and fair to see from; it has a population of seventy-five or eighty thousand, a famous college and a curious museum, many factories of cotton, porcelain and glass, foundries and flouring mills, and is the second city in point of wealth and importance in the Republic.

The only English speaking persons we met in Puebla, were the Rev. Mr. D——, a Protestant missionary from Ohio (for our introduction to whom we are indebted to Mrs. F——), and his wife. Mr. D——

told us I think that his congregation numbers one hundred and twenty-seven, twenty or more of whom are members of the orphanage, sustained by his Church. This seems a small number in so large a population, but he speaks hopefully and is zealous and earnest in his work.

We visited the marble works where the onyx marble is cut into slabs and other shapes and polished; there are some beautiful specimens being packed for the Paris exhibition and for England; we bought some table-tops to be sent after us.

The quarries are fifty miles off in Tecali and its neigbourhood, near the mountain el Pizarro. The marble seems identical with that found in Oran, in Algeria: it is translucent, and much of it is like moss agate.

9th March.

Mr. and Mrs. D—— were good enough to promise to engage carriages for the party, and to accompany us to Cholula, which is eight or nine miles off; at nine o'clock this morning we depart, the vehicles being two coaches and four, which Mr. D—— apologized for by the assurance that they will not cost more than coaches and two; and, certainly, the charge is small for them. The road is good, the day fine, a beautiful panorama is always before and about us, and everything is full of novelty and interest. We stop and get out at the foot of the great pyramid which is at the eastern end of the town of Cholula, though at one time in its centre. The pyramid is immense, but the traces of its once perfectly pyramidal shape are gone : it is misshapen and much serried and worn by the elements and other causes, its surface in many parts gone, and broken into holes. We ascended, following the path to the left, descending by that on the right, thus going round it. Its sides are full of trees, shrubs and plants, many of the former large and covered with flowers. On the top, where stood the Aztec temple and sacrificial stone, is a beautiful little church, gorgeously decorated, dedicated to the Virgen de los Remedios. [Don't be surprised, you have more than two thousand churches dedicated to the Blessed Virgin in England, not counting that of your own parish, Ste. Marie-la-bonne.] From its tower we could see what a large place Cholula has been : there were plainly visible all about and around, and very far from the present town, the lines and marks of the streets of the ancient city. In the time of Cortés it contained twenty thousand houses within its walls, and as many more in its suburbs : now the houses are a few hundreds

THE GREAT PYRAMID OF CHOLULA. 101

only, its population about eight thousand.* The height of the pyramid above the plain is about one hundred and eighty feet; the platform on its truncated summit is about an acre, and its square base covers a space of forty-four acres—a respectable mound indeed, for man's hands to make—but what a mere speck compared with the mighty mountains in the plain about it!

The pyramid is composed of layers of earth, adobe and burned brick.

We have with us a pleasing little book, written by Mr. Zabrinski Gray, who speaks of getting a curious old Aztec vase from "a woman of the country, a full-blooded Indian, presenting one of the

---

* The perpendicular height of the pyramid is 177 feet. Its base is 1,423 feet long, twice as long as that of the great pyramid of Cheops. . . . It reminds us of those colossal monuments of brick work which are still seen in ruins on the banks of the Euphrates, and in much higher preservation on those of the Nile.

On the summit stood a sumptuous temple, in which was the image of the mystic deity Quetzalcoatl, God of the air, with ebon features, unlike the fair complexion which he wore upon earth, wearing a mitre on his head waving with *plumes of fire*, with a resplendent collar of gold round his neck, pendants of mosaic turquoise in his ears, a jewelled sceptre in one hand, and a shield, curiously painted, the emblems of his rule over the winds, in the other. . . . . Nothing could be more grand than the view which met the eye from the area on the truncated summit of the pyramid. Towards the north stretched that bold barrier of porphyritic rock which nature has reared round the valley of Mexico, with the huge Popocatapetl and Iztaccihuatl standing like two colossal sentinels to guard the entrance to the enchanted region. Far away to the south was seen the conical head of Orizaba, soaring high into the clouds, and nearer, the barren, though beautifully shaped Sierra de Malinche, throwing its broad shadows over the plains of Tlascala.—PRESCOTT.

most perfect types of beauty it was ever his pleasure to behold." She was in a shop near the base of the pyramid, and "was a young creature of a loveliness that any land would be proud to possess, and a Raphael would be privileged to paint." We were anxious to get some relic from the pyramid—a vase like Mr. Gray's if possible, and to see the beauty he described, so we all go to the pulque shop, and find her sitting behind a counter with two pretty children. The only relic she can find for us is a rude, much-worn terra cotta mask, hideously ugly, which was dug up in her garden. She has very fine black eyes, like all the women of her race, but as to the rest, all I can say is we *tried* to agree with Mr. Gray. She gave us large tumblers of pulque which we tasted but could not swallow, it was so abominable. It seems a harmless drink, milky in appearance, and about as strong as weak cider.

Cholula has an immense public square, where Cortés perpetrated his great massacre in 1519. In this square is a large, strange Spanish Moorish old church, said to have been built by Cortés after the cathedral of Cordoba. It is low, very large, strangely decorated, and altogether something quite of itself and by itself. It is to be lamented that, like all the rest of Cholula, it is dirty, dilapidated and fast going into decay. Another church we went to see was a bright and only exception to all this. It had just been renovated, re-painted, frescoed and gilded. We went to get luncheon for our party where it had been ordered and partly prepared, but we were driven from the house by its unsavouriness; so we got some biscuits and fruit at a nondescript sort of shop, and, resuming our fours-in-hand, returned again past the great pyramid to Puebla.

We had often heard of Jalapa (pronounced "Halah-pa") as a place of great attraction and beauty, and read in the Spanish railway book on board ship that an Englishman who visited it for a day was so charmed with it that he never left it; also, that "its ladies are famed for their beauty and hospitality to strangers."

Of course we must go to Jalapa. It would be delightful to go across country to it from here, but we are told we should certainly be robbed, so the only alternative is to keep to the "ferro-carrill," the iron road, and to go round by Vera Cruz.

We leave Puebla with regret on Monday, the 11th March, at midnight, a favourite hour for starting trains in Mexico; but this gives us daylight to descend the mountains from Boca, which delight us as much as in our ascent. We get to Orizaba at half-past nine the next morning, and take up our old quarters in the hotel de diligentias.

The heat is much greater than when we were here last. A steamer leaves Vera Cruz for New Orleans on the 20th of March; another on the 15th of April. The coming heat, the intended sailing of the opera troupe in the latter, and her probably having to take soldiers to Matamoras, decide us to sail on the 20th of March.

13th March.

We bid adieu to Orizaba at ten this morning. At the station we were accosted by a very Spanish looking old gentleman, who turns out to be a Scotchman, or Scotch-Canadian, Dr. B———. He had lived, he said, many years in Canada, and was in Windsor, in 1838, when poor Dr. Hume of the Medical Staff, was brutally murdered and his body mangled by the pirates who attacked and burned it; some of these men, with swift justice, Colonel Prince "shot accordingly;" more of them were hanged in London a few weeks after. Of the many well-known Canadians of that time about whom Dr. B——— inquires, the only one yet alive is Dr. M——— of London, with whom he was at the Edinburgh University.

As the train stops at the station of Cordoba we get a good look at the town, and a good run about a garden above it. The town seems well built: there are many domes and spires, and the scenery about it is much like that about Orizaba, but the valley below it is more contracted. Vegetation is much more abundant and rich than there, and for an obvious reason—it is in the *tierras calientes*. Here, the scientific American sailor, Maury, successfully introduced the *quina* tree. The country in its neighbourhood produces enormous crops of tobacco, sugar and coffee. We intended to pay Cordoba a visit of two days, but deny ourselves the pleasure, as we are told the accommodation would be very indifferent; indeed it is doubtful whether we should get any. We descend the Chiquihuite mountains, cross the San Alejo and Chiquihuite bridges, with more barranca scenery, run through tunnels and come to Atoyac; here is a grand and lovely waterfall, and for some reason the train stops a couple of minutes just as we are above it, giving us a good view of it. Atoyac is less than fifteen hundred feet above the sea, and the heat manifestly increases as we approach the great sandy plain and its fever-giving marshes upon the sea side of which is Vera Cruz. We arrive at Vera

Cruz at five in the afternoon as we left it, in a sand storm, and put up at the Hotel Vera Cruzano, in order to be near the station, from which we depart at five to-morrow morning for Jalapa.

Some dinner and a long evening make us rather like Vera Cruz; *apropos* to the former, the fish called at New Orleans the red snapper is very abundant here, but far superior to his northern relations. I wish I could give you a bit of his tail, which is astonishingly the best part of him.

There are a great many public and private schools, two well sustained hospitals, and in what was the church of San Francisco, an excellent public library; water has been introduced from the Jamapa River, tending much to the health and cleanliness of the city, which contains within its walls 10,000 inhabitants, 4,000 outside them.

Education is compulsory here—think of that! The Legislature of the State of Vera Cruz, whose principal town this is, in 1873, declared "primary instruction and freedom of teaching to be obligatory," and ordered the establishment of one school for boys and another for girls, for each 2,000 inhabitants, and one for adults in every town of the State, and in each place of any industrial or commercial importance. The same law imposed upon the proper authorities, the obligation of establishing schools in jails and prisons, and *recommended* to landed proprietors and owners of factories and workshops, the adoption of a like system in their respective spheres, that the children of the day-labourers should partake of the benefits of primary instruction. To make obligatory education effective, penalties and rewards have been enacted, "the first consisting in the privation of certain offices and rights in regard to the fathers of families, who fail to comply with the law, the second limited to exemption from active service in the National Guard, and from the payment of any taxes arising therefrom."

We have admired the alameda and its rows of cocoa-trees, and the Indian laurels in the gardens of the plaza, and bought a lot of chocolate, famously good here, to take home with us.

The rest of the party have "retired," as our American cousins call going to bed, long since; and scribbling far into the night, I acknowledge to myself that the city of the "True Cross," or this its hotel, or both, are hot and stuffy.

Letter No. 7.

JALAPA, MEXICO,
17th March.

WE have been more than three days in this quiet old town, which is full of steep streets, stone houses, and flower gardens. It is within the district of country from whence comes *jalap*. The drug takes its name from the town, and is made from the turnip-like root of a large convolulus growing wild about here.

Jalapa contains 12,000 inhabitants, and is 4,350 feet above the sea. Its climate may be well put down as that of the temperate region; it is very healthy, and is much resorted to by invalids from the hot lands and coast. Town and country are full of flowers; even the little plaza in front of the cathedral has a garden, in which are some beautiful tropical flowers and shrubs, English roses, a pretty little fountain and pool. All this is public, and seemingly unguarded, for in Jalapa, as elsewhere in Mexico, flowers, trees, fountains, appear to be quite safe from vandalism. But I am getting on too rapidly. I am forgetting I have not brought *you* here yet, so let us go back to the Hotel Vera Crusano and Vera Cruz and my diary.

14th March.

We are called very early, get some coffee and a roll, and are at the station before five o'clock, to be stowed away, with a dozen other passengers, in a long, street-car sort of carriage, pulled, with two others in front of it, by a locomotive. We go on in the dark for an hour or so across the sandy desert when we reach Paso de San Juan, twenty miles, where some palm and other trees begin.

The air is sultry and heavy—indeed there seems no air. What there is of atmosphere depresses, loads and wearies us. The expedition at its commencement has almost made us ill. What an oven these hot lands must be in summer! Day begins to dawn, and we find Paso de San Juan has half-a-dozen houses, each consisting of little more than four posts and a roof of palm leaves. I dose my party, not forgetting myself, from a pannikin of weak brandy and water; considering the hour, it is very shocking, and is only mentioned in confidence, but it did us all much good—it was medicine.

Here the locomotive is exchanged for mules, and Mr. T——, the superintendent of the line hence to Jalapa, some fifty-three miles, greets us, and says, to our surprise, he has been expecting us, and has heard all about us.

We are packed into one of the carriages of the mule-train which is waiting for us, with a Jalapa lady, her two sons and little daughter.

The superintendent comes with us : he is full of conversation and information ; he, the daylight, the gradual ascent, fresher air, and the four mules pulling us along at a gallop, soon drive away our weariness and wretchedness.

Our fellow passengers are courteous and accommodating ; the mules are changed at reasonably short stages ; they gallop on the level, down-hill and round curves, which latter are sharp and frequent. Behind us comes a second-class carriage, and behind that another, with the baggage. All are four-in-hand. To look behind and see them galloping wildly after us suggests racing ; but there is nothing of the kind—it is all business.

Although Mr. T——'s attention is never off the railway and his work, he tells us so much about them and himself that, in three or four hours, we have all known him since the beginning of the

American war, by the afternoon, from his early boyhood. He is an old bachelor, and we cannot but sympathize with a man who, when he first came to the country, " knew no Spanish, to tell the beautiful Mexican señoritas how he loved them, and now that he knows the language, is too old," he says, " to think of anything of the kind."

About ten o'clock we pass an old Spanish fort, situated on a hill to our left, just above the river Antigua, a broad rapid jumping stream, with a very broken rocky bed. This we cross on a grand old stone bridge of many arches, formerly Puente del Rey, now, of course, Puente Nacional. Here was the scene of many an engagement between the troops of New and Old Spain in the long time of the revolutionary war, for it was a favourite spot for catching the silver on its way from the mines or mint to the coast. At the confluence of the Antigua with the sea was *old* Vera Cruz; but the river was not good for any purposes of navigation; it had an abominable bar, and so Vera Cruz was taken away and put where it is.

About six miles from Puente Nacional is Rinconada, where we find the happiness of plenty of cold water and towels; an excellent breakfast awaited us, put upon the table in a manner little to be expected in such a place, for, with the exception of the house we stop at, Rinconada is only a small collection of huts.

We do not see so much of green tropical foliage as we expected, the trees along the line being mostly deciduous, and it is only very early spring: many trees and shrubs, however, are clothed in their perpetual green, and some trees, without a single leaf on them, are covered with flowers. One tree, in particular, attracts our attention: it is loaded with large, beautiful, brilliantly red flowers. Mr. T—— says, in a couple of weeks, it will have so many more that there will be a compact mass of them impervious to the sun.

Inquiring in Mexico if this train carried any guard, I was answered, laughingly, "Oh, yes; there will be four or five rascals to take care of you."

I don't wish to be understood as applying that name to them, but certainly our guard does not *look* respectable, and I am sure no one of them "keeps a gig;" roughly, strangely clad, or half clad, they are a dangerous-*looking* lot, but, individually or collectively, strangely picturesque.

We pass some haciendas during the day, of which Mr. T—— gives us names and history: they are, some of them, very large estates, many leagues in length and breadth, but are only partially cultivated; indeed, we pass thousands of acres of uncultivated land, which need only to be *scratched* and planted to bring forth abundant crops in this climate; but when the crops come and are ready to be harvested it might be no one could be found to do the harvesting, for labour is hard to get, and lazy and uncertain when you get it hereabouts, and so much of this rich land is going back to its wild state. As we drive on, always ascending, we see in the woods right and left of us great numbers of the organ cactus, some of them forty, fifty and more feet high—graceful, slight green columns, running upwards straight as arrows. About eight miles (twelve and a half kilometros) from Rinconada we cross another river on a stone bridge of a single arch, and arrive at the village of Plan del Rio. This and Rinconada are the principal places on the road, but really they, like the others, possess little but their names. Wherever we change mules, there is a table covered with a white cloth placed by the road-side, on which are tortillas, sweet cakes and fruit, claret and other French wine, and good fresh cold water.

The tortilla is to the lower classes of Mexico what bread is to all ours. It is made from Indian corn, not ground, but soaked, and softened by soda or potash. Reduced to a pulpy substance, it is beaten and rolled by the Indian women into thin cakes, which are cooked in an earthen dish over a fire, generally of dried maguey leaves.

Here and there, we have come upon portions of large heavy paving, parts of the old paved road from Vera Cruz to Jalapa built by the Spaniards.

A little to the left, after passing Plan del Rio, we see a magnificent house and grounds, all going into disorder and decay. This was the hacienda of General Santa Anna, and the house was a palace built by him on it. Everything of any value about it that could be moved is gone. There were some beautiful marble seats about the grounds which, we are told, now ornament the plaza in Jalapa.

How often has Santa Anna's name been before the world, to disappear and reappear again and again, and what an eventful life was his! A brave soldier and able general, but unstable, and too ambitious of power and sway for himself, and too fond of money, he yet possessed immense influence over his countrymen. His greatest mistake was declaring himself President for life, with power to appoint his successor. The Mexican people wouldn't stand this and the rule that followed it, so there was another revolution. His last public act was his attack upon the Government of Juarez, in 1867, for which he was sentenced to death, but this was commuted, and he was exiled. On the death of Juarez he was permitted to return. He afterwards lived in seclusion in the City of Mexico, where he died about two years ago.

Our drive increases in beauty as the day wears on, and by three o'clock we have cool, refreshing air—we are in the mountain country.

Orizaba has been long in sight on our left, and we have now seen this great volcano, as we have the two others, from all points of view—we have seen all round them.

Soon a slight turn of the road brings another mountain into our view. It is very large and imposing; much nearer to us than Orizaba, but is without snow. It is the *Cofre de Perote*. Near to the foot of it is Jalapa, where we arrive at half-past four o'clock.

Leaving the railway-station we are guided up a steep street to an entrance which leads into the Hotel de Mexico. Within is a court-yard, as usual, open to the sky, surrounded with vases of plants and flowers. A large stone stair-case takes us to the next story, where are more plants and flowers and an aviary. We get good rooms, and there is promise of cleanliness, comfort and rest. And now, having brought you here, my dear A——, I can add we have had them all, and even some of that leisure which comes always in little retired places like Jalapa; but we have not been idle. We have been all round and about the town, and even ten miles out of it, to the Village of Coatepec, which is nothing of itself, but is beautifully situated in an undulating, fertile country. We went to it by a tram-road, worked by mules, up and down steeper hills and round sharper curves than ever tram-road traversed before. The mules were poor, half-starved—a sad contrast to those which brought us from Vera Cruz on the English Railway Company's line, which were well cared for under the eye of their superintendent, and saved from the ill-treatment these poor brutes suffer. And to-day three of our party dined with the superintendent, meeting Mr. T—— and his beautiful bride, to whom we had been introduced in Mexico. He is a Director of the Railway Company, and is here, on its business, on his way to England.

But we have *not* ascended the *Cofre de Perote*, although we are just under it. I have already given you my humble sentiments about getting up mountains, and this one is far above the line I drew. It is 13,552 feet high, including the *cofre*, the trunk or box-shaped monolinth of rock, standing erect outside and above its summit, from which the Spaniards gave it its name. The ancient name of the mountain, *Nauhcampateptl*, signifying quadrangular mountain, was given to it probably for the same reason. *Perote* is the plateau of country lying between the two volcanic chains of Popocatapetl and Orizaba, which strike north and south.

Humboldt, whose measurement I give you, and who, of course, knew most about it, says this immense rock is of pumice (probably dark porphyritic pumice, hence its being called *porphyry* in all the books but his), and that it was carried up during the upheaval of the mountain. He instances a similar phenomenon as having occurred in Vesuvius in 1834.*

There was a large convent of Franciscan monks here until the law abolished them; this convent, which is a very fine building, and the cathedral are the most noteworthy buildings. Both are said to have beeen commenced by Cortés.

We have been to the market again and again, and are never tired of looking at the two or three hundred Indians, men and women, who attend it, with

---
* 5 Cosmos, 326 n.

fruit, wild roots, flowers, vegetables, shawls, serapes, &c.

We got some arrowroot from them, which, cooked as a vegetable, is very good.

Apropos to the Indians, I don't think either I or T—— have told you what *serapes, rebosos,* or *tilmas* are. The serape may be merely a blanket with a hole for the head to go through, but it is often of very fine wool, or mixed wool and cotton, and striped in bright colours. The reboso in use is the female serape; it is a long shawl of fine cotton, very neatly made by the Indian women, and ornamented at the ends with net-work and fringes, sometimes of silk. In warm weather they wear it hanging over the arm, in cold weather wrapped gracefully around the head, with one end thrown over the shoulder.

The *tilmatli* of the Aztecs, or the *tilma,* as it is now called, is a square, short cloak, made to tie at the ends across the breast or over one shoulder.

Nor have I told you of the beautiful feather and wax work we saw in Mexico. You read much of the Aztec's art in the former in Prescott, and they possess it still. Little specimens of their skill in feather-work and drawing combined, in the shape of sketches of birds and flowers on cards finished with feathers are very common, and many were brought to the hotel for sale. Their wax-work would make Madame Tussaud die of envy if she hadn't died long ago. The little figures of caballero and steed, of the water-seller, the charcoal-seller, of every other street-crier are perfect—no sculptor, no painter could do them better, and they are got up and dressed to the very life. We are loaded with them.

Jalapa becomes more and more pleasing. It grows upon us, and if I were satisfied that walks and drives for some miles about it were quite safe, we should make a much longer stay here. If it has a fault, it is that its climate is too rainy; the clouds are caught between sea and table land by the Cofre, and made to discharge—hence its many flowers and rich vegetation. We have had much rain during our stay, and I have made a calculation, from this and other data, that the rainfall in Jalapa is about one-fourth that of England, and one-sixth that of Ireland.

I hope I may not be cross-examined on this statement, for, though I think I have nearly hit the truth, the reasons for my conclusions may not hold water.

In one of our walks, we passed a music school in

full operation—I am not punning—and stopping to listen to its sweet sounds, were invited to come in by the master. We stayed within some time, and were much gratified by the skill, voice and taste displayed. Master and pupils were all Indians.

Jalapa, like Cordoba, is very Spanish. Balconies are numerous, and the latticed iron cage outside the windows as common here as there. Both these, by-the-way, have a good deal to do with Mexican courtships and marriages—in the towns at all events. The various ways and means used in England, Canada, &c., of man's paying his addresses to woman, the "courting," "sweet-hearting," "sparking," "keeping company," &c., would not be tolerated. When a gentleman has serious intentions towards a lady, he shows himself in the street near her balcony or window, casting continual and most respectful glances at it; if he can, *looking* love. This is unheeded for a time, but, often repeated, it generally softens the *senorita's* heart, and she appears at balcony or window for a moment; the lover, thus encouraged, comes again and again, each time *drawing* the lady, who lingers longer and longer, that he may gaze at her, and she see more of him. Whether there is any dumb show or striking of attitudes I was not told, but no word is spoken, at all events, so far as the outside world knows. A crisis comes in these performances, in which there is either parental interference or parental consent, in which latter case the parties are never permitted to be together, or to enjoy the romance and sweets of courtship in each other's society, or to discuss their future; all *that* has to wait for the marriage, which follows this singular beginning. But there is never any doubt as to what this beginning means; it is never, like chops and tomato sauce, or the harmless attentions and conversations of intentionless gentlemen to pleasing ladies elsewhere, liable to misconstruction.

We have not met the Englishman who could not tear himself away from Jalapa, nor have we seen the ladies or any of them " famed for their beauty and hospitality to strangers;" but the husband of the lady, our fellow-passenger from Vera Cruz, has, in Spanish fashion, placed " his house, his servants, mules and carriages at my service: they are all mine."

I don't know who would be the more embarrassed, he or I, if I took him at his word.

March 18.

We leave Jalapa this morning with much regret

and some serious thought of another visit to it some day. We have Orizaba in sight for nearly thirty miles of our way: what a glorious mountain it is, and how immensely higher it looks than when we first saw it! The reason is simply that our first view was when we were up close to the table land from whence it springs; now we are low down in the hot lands. The day is beautifully clear, and we see far up its sides from its base many shades of green, which we are told are mostly dense pine forest; above this the coloring is gray and brown, and then the snow and ice to the peak top, fascinating to look at, but dazzling to the eyes in this bright sun. According to Messieurs Doighon and Huerta, who ascended it, the crater is 6,000 yards in circumference (nearly three and a half miles); its diameter from north to south 2,500 yards; from east to west, 1,500 yards.

At Rinconada an excellent luncheon is awaiting us, and we get an hour's rest. Mr. and Mrs. T——, with the superintendent lead our line of carriages: we go down much faster than we came up, and as we descend the heat becomes hotter and hotter.

We find vegetation has much increased, spring advanced along the whole line of road during our few days' absence: going up we saw innumerable round bunches of what seemed dry sticks in the trees, which I took for birds' nests, so like were they to the rooks' nests in English elms; coming back, they are clusters of beautiful buds and flowers—they are *orchids*.

We arrive at Vera Cruz at 5 p.m., and at the station Mr. T——, the superintendent, has to say good-bye to us. He is a genial warm-hearted Southerner, and we shall not soon forget the kindness he has shown us, though it is rendered perhaps, not so much on our own accounts as because we are passengers of the company he serves.

Vera Cruz, everybody said, possessed no carriages of any kind, but a ricketty vehicle with a pair of much worn mules presented itself at the Hotel Vera Cruzano. The driver refused to take any luggage, and, carrying three of the party to the Hotel de Mexico, something over 200 yards, demanded four dollars, and would make no abatement. I wanted to pay him to avoid any annoyance, but Van W——, who had offered him two dollars, refused to do it. The result was the man got nothing, for we heard no more of him. I much wished to get on board the ship to-night, but it is out of the question, as there has been a "norther," and the sea is beating heavily over the mole still.

Really Vera Cruz seems *not* what it is represented to be. There is no sickness in it now. It has baths, water-works, gas, and the *sapilotes* (buzzards) carry off and devour all the refuse which the inhabitants leave at their doors for them. I saw these birds doing this with as much deliberation as if they were unfeathered scavengers, but, of course, they took the choice pieces first.

The town looks clean and bright as we walk about in the late evening, and sounds of pleasing music mingle with the beating of the surf. There is a bright moon, and everything seems to bear witness that the bad name given to the place in former days is no longer merited: but I mean to get out of it as soon as I can.

We are at the Hotel de Mexico, which is crowded, and so we have rooms at the top of the house— perhaps all the better for us, as they are more airy than below. The rooms on the sea side have a pleasant air in them; on the other side *they have not*.

Heat and a deficient mosquito net keep me, but happily not the rest of the party, awake nearly all night, during the latter part of which I hear a man, not many rooms away, retching violently.

Elsewhere I should have promptly set this down to the patient having gone to bed "half-seas over," and that he was very ill from it, and it served him right; but the darkness, heat, mosquitoes, and the *venue being Vera Cruz*, all tended to another conclusion: it could only be *el vomito*, and all the pleasant appearances of last evening were *mere* appearances,—the demon, not of drunkenness, but of yellow fever, was here still! Drowsily thinking all this over and over again, sleep came and took it away from me.

March 19.

A bright, lovely morning, and so clear and fresh: they say it is always clear before a "norther" tho'—I wonder if another is coming. The day is charming, and no thought of the noises in the night disturb the enjoyment of it.

But my purpose to get on board ship remains unchanged, though there is not that unanimity I expected among my party on that question. "It is so nice here, and we want to shop; and what is the good of going to the ship the day before she sails?" is put forward more than once, to meet with this answer: "The ship is safe, the city may not be; it is smooth water, and that may not last long; we will go now." So the shopping is hurried, last looks are taken at plaza and trees, bags are packed, and rooms left to be returned to no more.

I should like to telegraph to Canada by way of New Orleans, but the line is out of order, again the monkeys have broken the wires.

By noon we are clear of hotel and custom-house, and taking a boat, are soon with all our impedimenta again on board the good steam-ship *City of Mexico*, and re-possessed of our old state rooms.

We sail to-morrow for New Orleans.

Letter No. 8.

S.S. CITY OF MEXICO, VERA CRUZ HARBOUR,
March 20.

WHEN I finished my last letter to you yesterday, I had no idea of beginning another here; but I have more leisure than I can employ, and am likely to have much more before we sail; when that is to be no one can say at present.

Waking about one this morning, I stepped out of my cabin, which is on deck, to look at the night, and was staggered and all but thrown down by the wind, of which I had had no suspicion, so soundly had I slept.

A "norther" had come, and was in full blast. We were tearing at our anchors; just a-head of us was a great lump of a brig with her stern, on which was painted "*Sarah Fraser, Portland,*" within seventy yards or so of us. She was tearing at her anchors too, and at her every rise I expected her to be upon us. On our right, about two hundred yards or so behind us, was an American man-of-war, tearing at *her* anchors. All round us, outside the space where was anchorage and absence of surf,—in a word, outside the harbour were shoals of coral reef covered with raging, leaping, flying surf: one of these about three hundred yards behind, and directly to leeward of us, was *la lavendera* (the washerwoman), upon which no ship could hold together half an hour. Connecting the brig, ourselves, and this abominable shoal rapidly in my mind, I thought how very *de trop* the *Sarah Fraser* was, *where* she was; that if her cable parted, as it might at any moment, she would instantly be down upon us with a blow and a weight so immense that we should part *our* cable too, and off we should both go to *la lavendera*.

The "norther" certainly was, and as I write is, tremendous; but, comparing it with the gales of the North Atlantic, I should say *they* were much more mighty and frightful.

What impressed me most during my first few minutes on deck was—first, our very uncomfortable surroundings, and next the unearthly, fiendish *hiss* of the "norther." I never heard anything in gale or hurricane like it, and until the ear became a little accustomed to it it was really terrifying.

But with all this, what a beautiful scene it was! There was the clearest sky and the brightest moon that ever shone, lighting up everything from the fairy-looking sleeping city to the painted name on the stern of the brig. Away before us on our right was the Castle of San Juan d'Ulloa, looking as it never looks in daylight: close under its lee were some small craft snugly placed, and to the left and far in front of us was a big Liverpool steamer, like ourselves, riding out the gale. Captain McIntosh, our excellent captain, was on deck, and I had an hour's chat with him. I suggested he ought to have steam up, but he said he didn't think the weather was bad enough. I didn't believe him, and had no doubt he had already given the order for it; and I was right, for not an hour after, our steam *was* up, and I went to bed again with no more anxieties about *la lavendera* or the *Sarah Fraser*.

21st March.

We had the "norther" all day yesterday, our sailing day, in its full violence; it blows still, but is more subdued. We shall probably not sail till late to-morrow, by which time the sea will be down sufficiently to enable us to get our passengers and freight.

I

This afternoon, Captain B—— of the United States frigate O—— came on board with Dr. T——, the surgeon of his ship. We learn from them that the cable of their best and holding anchor parted before daylight yesterday morning, and but for having steam up they would have gone on the shoals; but men of war are never caught napping in this respect.

Captain B—— is sailor-like, brusque, chatty; Dr. T——, like all naval surgeons whom I have met, is travelled and well read.

The war which threatens the peace of all Europe inevitably comes into our conversation, and Captain B—— imparts to me his settled conviction that England will soon be at war with Russia and some other Power, probably Prussia, and *" then will come the Battle of Dorking !"*

He says this with no air of sadness or solemnity befitting the thought of such a catastrophe and its consequences to all the world, but rather with one of elation and gladness, which surprises me, for I have long believed that if there were haters of England among the Americans, even they would not like to see her " whipped " by anybody but themselves.

I humbly suggest that the " Battle of Dorking "

was only written to frighten England out of her Volunteer system; that it is never likely to occur, and that besides she has ridden out many storms more dangerous than the present one, and will live and flourish long after this is over.

These gentlemen remain on board to dinner, and the consequence to me is a very pleasing two hours' conversation with them.

Speaking of the ruins of ancient buildings in Mexico, Dr. T—— tells us that there lives in Vera Cruz a Mexican gentleman who has made the antiquities of his country his especial study; that he has deciphered the inscriptions found at Palenque, Uxmal, and other places; that he has discovered that the Aztec calendar stone built into the cathedral at Mexico is only calculated and intended for half the year, and that he found the stone for the other half in the woods near Tuxpan, imbedded in the earth; that he has many curious manuscripts and other relics connected with the ancient history of the country, and if I land to-morrow an hour's talk with him may be attainable.

Continuing the subject of these ruins, Dr. T—— adds that the Emperor Maximilian had some very fine large photographs of them taken by a Parisian artist whom he sent to them for the purpose with a strong guard, and that Dr. Trowbridge, the United States Consul at Vera Cruz, has some of these photographs in his possession.

22nd March.

The "norther" has passed away, but there is still a good deal of sea. About 11 o'clock I manage to get ashore, and, hastening to the United States Consulate, have the good fortune to find Dr. Trowbridge, the Consul, disengaged. I tell him the object of my visit, and in a moment a number of large beautiful photographs are placed before me. They are numbered, have their titles in French, and the names "Charnay, photogr. Gide, editeur, Paris," at the foot, in the left-hand corner of each. The execution is beautiful, and their subjects have long been matter of great interest to me. The Consul tells me I may take them away with me, and have as many copies taken as I like, returning him the originals and one copy for himself. I gladly accept his terms, and he leaves the room for a few minutes while I am devouring the photographs, which I can hardly believe I may carry off.

It occurs to me, what an impressively respectable appearance I must have! Here am I, a stranger, a foreigner, suddenly entrusted with property of great value and beauty by a gentleman who never before saw or heard of me. But the Consul soon returns and scatters this vanity to the winds. He brings a small packet of handkerchiefs which Mrs. F—— has been kind enough to send for T—— to his care, and that packet is the sole and only reason for his trust in me.*

He tells me that Señor J. M. Melgar is the *savant* whom I seek; that he possesses more knowledge than any one else of ancient Mexico, all acquired in the country by severe study, labour and research, and that he is an honorary member of, and has medals from, several learned societies of Spain and France.

The Consul knows him very well: he confirms what Dr. T—— says of him, and adds what I almost fear to write, it is so at variance with all I have read on the subject, that Señor Melgar declares all the old Toltec inscriptions are partly or wholly in Egyptian character, or in a character very similar.

---

* I was for some time under the impression that these photographs had never been published, but I see in Mr. Baldwin's "Ancient America," mention is made of "a recent French volume by Desiré Charnay, which is accompanied by a folio volume of photographs." Although I miss the name of Gide, I infer that this *folio* contains all the photographs, part of which only I obtained.

Messrs. Stanton and Vicars, of Toronto, copied them most admirably for me.

He is eccentric and difficult to find at short notice, and with much regret I have to give up the prospect of seeing him; but I hope yet to find in print the information he must have given to the societies whose medals he bears.* Returning to

---

* My copy of "Ancient America" is old—1872. Finding no word of Señor Melgar's discoveries in it, I sent for the last edition (1878), but found that was only a reprint of the first. Anxious for further information about them, I addressed a letter to the Hon. Mr. Baldwin, informing him of all I had heard, and begging him to tell me if he had any knowledge of them, and what he thought of them, adding he might be assured I would make no use of his reply without his authority, and inclosing my card. I felt I was as much doing a service as seeking a favour; but I fear Mr. Baldwin thinks otherwise, and that my addressing him even on a subject so interesting to himself and his many readers, however courteously it was done, was, in his judgment, a liberty not to be taken by a stranger, for my letter has not been noticed. I do not, however, regret my *sin*, as, at all events, my information is in good hands: if it be worth anything it will bear fruit.

With better success, I wrote to the Consul at Vera Cruz for more information on the subject, and with a request that search might be made to complete the set of photographs.

To-day (22nd Aug., 1879), just as I am sending these last sheets off to the press, I receive the following kind letter in reply:—

"U. S. CONSULATE, VERA CRUZ,
"Aug. 9, 1879.

"Mr. H. C. R. BECHER,
"Thornwood, London, Canada.

"DEAR SIR,— Yours of 25th June came to my office while I was visiting the Capitol, and hence is delayed the answer.

"Mr. Melgar is not here now, but I will give you what I have heard and what I believe to be true:

"He is an hon. member of the Archæological Societies of London and Paris, and has medals for original investigations from both. The other half of the calendar stone (the first half being at the Cathedral in Mexico City) was found by Senor Mulgar a few leagues back of Mizantla, near Tuxpan— *i.e.*, Mizantla is near Tuxpan. Melgar has no theory that I have heard of as to how the stones (calendar) were separated, if ever in the same vicinity. There are noble ruins in the neighbourhood of Mizantla, and the calendar is still among them.

the ship, I find that Captain B—— has carried off my party and some other ladies in his gig to luncheon. Upon their return, they are warm in their praises of the hospitality and courtesy of their host and his officers. All our passengers are on board, among them some nice people from New York and Utica, and at two o'clock, although it is Friday, we sail for New Orleans.

23rd March.

We pass the wreck of the *Havana* again, and anchor off Tuxpan, which we leave at 2 p.m.

During our stay here we saw a large shark playing about the ship with nearly the quickness of a trout; salt pork, with a hook and chain, in a minute from its touching the water, bring about his suspension at the ship's side. They want to get his liver, that being worth money, but don't seem to know how to do it; the quarter-master stands on the chain that holds the monster, and has a knife between his teeth for the purpose, but his foothold

---

" As to the last links in the photos., I have tried to restore them, but have as yet failed. Should I be able to get the completed set, will not forget to send you the missing numbers. I thank you for the interest you have given to these photos., and hope I may have the pleasure of reading your book on this interesting country.

" With my kindest regards, I am, dear sir,
" Yours respectfully,
" S. T. TROWBRIDGE."

is so unsteady he does not use it, and every moment I expect to see him fall down the shark's throat, which is wide open. A large boat full of Aztecs comes alongside, and the shark is handed over to their tender mercies. They know what to do ; he is floated alongside them, his head held well up by the chain and hook ; one of them opens a big clasp knife, cuts a line some five feet long or so in the shark's side, out come three or four bushels of liver, &c., which are carefully stowed in the boat, the hook is removed from his mouth, and the shark sinks to swim no more.

Scarcely was this shark disposed of, when another was hooked in the same way, and suspended from the ship's side ; the boat full of Mexicans had gone, so the crew had to deal with him. We heard of countless shots from passengers' revolvers being fired into his head, without making him move his horrible eyes ; of immense bare beef-bones, large stones, and some half-digested fish being taken from his stomach, and that he, like the other, was thirteen feet and some inches long.

Sunday, 24th March.

We arrived off Tampico, where it is very hot, at five this morning, and sail again at 2 p.m. with fruit, vegetables, turtle, and many fowls and turkeys added to our stock. I have omitted to tell you that the distance on our course between Vera Cruz and New Orleans is nine hundred miles.

I must now make some mention of a subject to which I have scarcely alluded. Perhaps Mexico was never so free from robbery and brigandage as it now is, but the material for both are present in city and country, and both exist. All who come here should take heed of where they go, and of the hour of their going and staying, and ask for information in all proper quarters, especially if ladies are of the party.

I took care never to be far off the rail or tramways unless in much frequented thoroughfares, and by daylight; the occasion of our drive from Puebla to Cholula, and the returning from parties at night, half a mile or so from our hotel in the City of Mexico, were the only exceptions to this rule, but I was never without some anxiety on the subject, having ladies with me, and was always circumspect and watchful.

It was during the French occupation that brigandage most flourished. The diligences between Vera Cruz and Mexico were frequently stopped and the passengers stripped of all their money and valuables by one set of miscreants, and then again stopped by another set, who would beat them for parting with the riches they had lost, and then take from them every shred of their clothing. It was no uncommon thing to see the diligence stop before an hotel in the City of Mexico and the passengers rush from it, with blanket or newspaper—anything to hide their want of garments. If we are to believe what travellers say, the danger of being robbed and ill-treated is still great, but it is apparent that the present government is doing all it can to put the trouble down with a strong hand and quick justice.

March 26th.

We got into the Mississippi, by the South Pass, at five this morning, just escaping a severe gale, or rather its effects at sea, for it follows us up the river all the way to New Orleans. We are again gratified with the perfume of orange blossoms; there are hundreds of trees full of fruit and flower along the banks of the river.

At six o'clock we arrive at New Orleans, and find awaiting us a heap of letters from England, India, and Canada.

So the Mexican part of our outing is over, leaving us many regrets that it is over. But we have yet more than a month on our hands in which we can get a good rest here, and then take a leisurely look at the Southern States, including Florida.

We have been much pleased during our stay here to receive a visit from Colonel F—— the United States Minister to Mexico, now on his way there.

He was good enough to take some trouble to find us out at the St. Charles, and through his kind thought we are invited to visit the beautiful club-house and gardens of the Louisiana Jockey Club.

We left New Orleans on the 4th of April, visiting Montgomery, Atlanta, Augusta, and Savannah. From the latter place we went South again, to Florida, by the Inland Navigation route.

We went to Fernandina, where, by the way, is a beautiful new hotel, to Jacksonville, and then up the St. John River, and by rail to St. Augustine.

Having seen enough of Florida, we returned to Savannah, and from there we went to Charleston, Wilmington, Richmond, White Sulphur Springs, Staunton, Harper's Ferry, Washington, and Baltimore.

From Baltimore we came to the Falls of Niagara by Harrisburgh, Williamsport, Watkyn's Glen, and Rochester.

At the Falls of Niagara we stayed two or three

days at Clark Hill, which overlooks the rapids and Horse-shoe Fall. This morning, the 29th April, at ten o'clock, we left the Falls, and at two this afternoon our trip is over, we are again at home.

We have been absent eleven weeks, have travelled some six thousand miles, and have had a very enjoyable outing. The Mexican part of it was simply delightful, and we shall always have pleasing memories of it. But after it all we better appreciate our own home and Dominion. Taking Canada all in all, we think we have seen no state or country in our tour that is preferable or equal to it. If its winters are a little too long, its summers too hot, its climate is, perhaps, the most healthful and enjoyable in the world, and it makes its people strong, hardy, energetic.

In it life and property are safe; the law is always supreme and carried out by its own officers; the people God fearing, law-abiding.

The Government is the freest in the world—like that of England, directly from the people; and here, as there, no Ministry can stand a day that is not supported by a majority of them through their representatives in Parliament. There is no theory that all men are equal, but an unwritten one, truer better, well understood and never lost sight of in practice, that the *rights* of all men are equal.

From north to south, from the Atlantic to the Pacific, Canada has untold wealth in soil, forests, rivers, lakes, fisheries, coal, mines, minerals, metals. True to itself, it has a glorious future before it, and though last, not least, if politics run high, and *Grit* and *Conservative* continually forget they are men and brethren, these parties alike, with all its people, have a love for it, for their Sovereign and the *Old Country*, with which they are happily connected, that speaks, strongly and unmistakeably, of their contentment, their appreciation of the blessings they enjoy, and their desire for their perpetuation.

APPENDIX.

A paper about the ancient nations and races who inhabited Mexico before and at the time of the Spanish Conquest; and the ancient stone and other structures, and ruins of ancient cities found there.

THE mountainous region of Mexico, like the Caucasus, was inhabited from the most remote period by a great number of nations of different races.

The most ancient nations of Mexico, those who considered themselves as *autochthones*, are the Olmecs, or Hulmecs, the Xicalancs, the Cores, the Tepanecs, the Tarascs, the Miztecs, the Tzapotecs, and the Otomites.

The Olmecs and the Xicolancs, who inhabited the elevated plain of Tlascala, boasted of having vanquished or destroyed, on their arrival, the giants, or *quinametin*; a tradition founded probably on the appearances of the fossil bones of elephants found in those elevated regions of the mountains of Anahuac.

The Toltecs, migrating from their country, Huehuetlapallan, or Tlapallan, in the year 544 of our era, arrive at Tollantzinco, in the country of Anahuac, in 648, and at Tula in 670.

Under the reign of the Toltec king Ixtilcuechahuac, in 708, the astrologer Huematzin composed the celebrated *Divine Book*, the *Teoamoxtli*, which contained the history, the mythology, the calendar, and the laws of the nation.

The Toltecs also appear to have constructed the pyramid of Cholula, on the model of the pyramids of Teotihuacan, which last are the most ancient of all; and Siguenza believes them to be the work of the Olmecs.

It was in the time of the Toltec monarchy, or in the ages anterior to it, that the Mexican Buddha, *Quetzalcohuatl*, appeared; a white man, bearded, and accompanied by other strangers, who wore black garments in the form of cassocks. Till the 16th century, the people wore these dresses to disguise themselves in festivals. The name of this saint was *Cuculea*, in Yucatan, and *Camaxtli* at Tlascala. His cloak was spotted with red crosses. High priest of Tula, he founded religious congregations. He ordained sacrifices of flowers and fruit, and stopped his ears when he was spoken to of war. His fellow-adventurer *Huemac* was in possession of the secular authority, while he himself enjoyed the spiritual power. This form of government was similar to those of Japan and of Cundinamarca; but the first monks, Spanish missionaries, have gravely discussed the question whether Quetzalcohuatl was a Carthaginian, or an Irishman. From Cholula he sent colonies to Mixteca, Huaxayacac, Tabasco and Campeachy. It is supposed that the palace at Milta was built by order of this unknown personage. At the time of the arrival of the Spaniards, certain green stones which had belonged to him, were preserved as precious relics at Cholula; and F. Torribio de Motilinia beheld sacrifices offered in honour of the Saint on the summit of the Mountain Matlalcuyc, near Tlascala.

The same monk was present at Cholula at ceremonies ordered by Quetzalcohuatl, in which the penitents sacrificed their tongue, ears, and lips. The high priest of Tula had made his first appearance at Panuco. He left Mexico with the intention of returning to Tlapallan, and it was in this journey that he disappeared, not in the north as might have been supposed, but in the east, on the banks of the Rio Huasacualco. The nation expected his return during a number of ages.*

In 1051 pestilence and destruction of the Toltecs.

They push their migration further to the South.

Two children of the last king, and some Toltec families remain in the country of Anahuac.

In 1170 the Chichemecs, issuing from their country Amaquemacan, arrive in Mexico.

In 1178 migration of the Nahuatlacs (Anahuatlacs). This nation contained the seven tribes of Sochimilcs, Chalcs, Tepanecs, Acolhuans, Tlahuics, Tlascaltecs, or Tesochichimecs, and Aztecs, or Mexicans, who, as well as the Chichimecs, *all spoke the Toltec language.*

These tribes called their country Aztlan, or Teo-Acolhuacan, and declared it to be near Amaquemacan.

The Aztecs had migrated from Aztlan, according to Gama, in 1064; according to Clavigero, in 1160. The Mexicans, properly so called, separated themselves from the Tlascaltecs and the Chalcs in the mountains of Zacatecas.

In 1087 the Aztecs arrive at Tlaxixco or Acahualtzinco; reform of the Calendar, and first festival of the new fire since the going out from Aztlan in 1091.

---

* The Druses, who became a distinct sect about the close of the tenth century, believe that Hakim, whose soul is in China, will come back in about 900 years, so that he may be expected at any moment. See an article entitled "Syria, among the Druses," in Blackwood's, Sept. 1879.

Arrival of the Aztecs at Tula in 1196, at Tzompanco in 1216, and at Chapultepec in 1245.

Under the reign of Nopaltzin, King of the Chichimecs, a Toltec called Xiuhtlato, lord of Quauhtepec, taught the people, about the year 1250, the culture of maize and cotton, and the making of bread from the flour of maize. The small number of Toltec families that dwelt along the banks of the Lake Tenochtitlan, had entirely neglected the culture of this grain, and the American corn would have been for ever lost if Xiuhtlato had not preserved a few seeds from his early youth.

Union between the three nations of the Chichimecs, the Acolhuans and the Toltecs, by matrimonial alliances of members of the royal families of each.

Few nations exist whose annals offer so great a number of names of families, and places, as the hieroglyphic annals of Anahuac.

The Mexicans fall under the yoke of the Acolhuans in 1314, but soon succeed in freeing themselves by their valour.

Foundation of Tenochtitlan in 1325.

List of Mexican Kings given, eleven in number, from Acamapitzin 1352 down to Guatemozin 1521, when Cortes took the City of Tenochtitlan."

Abridged from a "fragment" written by Humboldt, and appearing in the "Vues des Cordillères et monumens des peuples indigènes de l'Amerique." Vol. 2, p. 385. (Note wherever Humboldt is again referred to, this work is intended.)

Humboldt, in the fragment I have partly quoted, alludes to the death during the reign of one of the Mexican kings, about the year 1470, of Nezahualcoyotl, a King of Acolhuacan, or Tezcuco, "equally memorable for the improvement of his mind and the wisdom of his legislation." He speaks of his having composed, in the Aztec language, sixty hymns in honour of the Supreme Being; an elegy on the destruction of a city, and another on the instability of human greatness. He adds that the great botanist Hernandez had made use of several of the drawings of plants and animals, with which this king had ornamented his palace in Tezcuco, and which had been made by Aztec painters.

The Acolhuans, it will be remembered, belonged to the same family with the Aztecs: they built their capital, Tezcuco, on the eastern end of the lake, opposite to that on which the Aztecs founded theirs, and were thereafter generally called Tezcucans.

It was in the reign of this king that the remarkable league of unity was formed between the three powers of Tezcuco, Mexico and Tlacopan, another state bordering on the lake, which existed at the time of the Spanish invasion, and during his reign and that of his son and successor, Nezahualpili, was what Prescott calls the "Golden Age of Tezcuco."

The Tepanecs invaded the territory of the Tezcucans in 1418, took

K

Tezcuco, killed the king, and subjugated his kingdom. Nezahualcoyotl, heir to the crown, and then fifteen years old, witnessed his father's death, while he lay concealed among the branches of a tree. His subsequent history, says Prescott, from whom I learn what I am about to say of him, is "as full of romantic daring, and perilous escapes, as that of the renowned Scanderbeg, or of the young Chevalier."

Soon after his father's death he fell into the hands of the Tepanecs and was thrown into a dungeon. Effecting his escape, through the connivance of the governor of the fortress, an old servant of his family, who took the place of the royal fugitive, and paid for his loyalty with his life, he was at length permitted, through the intercession of the reigning family in Mexico, which was allied to him, to retire to their capital. Here he remained for eight years pursuing his studies under an old preceptor, who had had the care of his early youth.

The Tepanec usurper dying, bequeathed the Empire to his son Maxtla, a man of fierce and suspicious temper. On his succession, Nezahualcoyotl hastened to pay his obeisance to him, but the tyrant refused the little present of flowers laid at his feet, and turned his back on him in presence of his chieftains. Soon the prince's life became one of flight and hiding. Attempts were made by Maxtla to assassinate him. Whoever should take him dead or alive, was promised, however humble his degree, the hand of a noble lady and an ample domain. But the love borne him by his subjects, and indeed by some of the troops sent in search of him, was proof against all this. Soon the aggressive nature of Maxtla had caused alarm among the neighbouring states, who formed a coalition, and on an appointed day Nezahualcoyotl found himself at the head of a force sufficiently strong to put down the invaders. He entered the capital of his country and was received as its lawful king.

Soon he united his forces with the Mexicans, and, after some bloody battles, the usurper, Maxtla, was completely routed. He fled to the baths, whence he was dragged out, and sacrificed with the usual cruel ceremonies of the Aztecs.

The restored monarch remodelled the various departments of his government.

He framed a code of laws so well suited to the exigencies of the times that it was adopted by the two other powers of the league, Mexico and Tlacopan. It was written in blood, and entitled the author, Prescott says, to be called the Draco rather than the "Solon of Anahuac," as he is fondly styled by his admirers.

He divided the government among a number of departments, the council of war, the council of finance, the council of justice. This last was supreme, both in civil and criminal matters, receiving appeals from the lower tribunals of the provinces, which were obliged every eighty days to make reports of their proceedings.

In all these bodies a certain number of citizens were allowed to have seats with the nobles and professionals.

There was a council of state for aiding the king in the dispatch of business, and advising him in matters of importance, drawn altogether from the highest chiefs ; it was of fourteen members, and they had seats provided at the royal table.

Lastly, there was the council of music, which, differing from the import of its name, was devoted to science and art. Works on anatomy, chronology, history, or any other science were submitted to its judgment before they could be made public.

The wilful perversion of truth in history was made a capital offence ; and this body drawn from the best instructed persons had the supervision of all the productions of art, and the nicer fabrics. It decided on the qualifications of the professors in the various branches of science, the fidelity of their instruction, the deficiency of which was severely punished, and it instituted examinations of these latter. In short it was a responsible board of education for the country. On stated days compositions and poems were recited before it by their authors. Seats were provided for the three crowned heads of the empire, who deliberated with the other members on the merits of the pieces, and distributed prizes to the successful competitors.

Such are the marvellous accounts transmitted to us of this institution—one calculated to give, says Prescott, a higher idea of the refinement of the people, than even the noble architectural remains which still exist. The archives, which were in the royal palace, were stored with the records of primitive ages.

In one of Nezahualcoyotl's odes, he says : " Banish care, there are bounds to pleasure ; the saddest life must also have an end. Weave the chaplet of flowers, and sing thy songs and praise to the all-powerful God ; for the glory of the world soon fadeth away. . . . Yet the remembrance of the just shall not pass from the nations, and the good thou hast done shall ever be held in honour. The goods of this life, its glories and its riches, are but lent to us ; its substance is but an illusory shadow, and the things of to-day shall change on the coming of the morrow."

But the Tezcucan monarch, although a bard, did not pass all his hours in dalliance with the muse: he encouraged agriculture and war, and in early manhood practised the latter to the increase of the area, and the population of his country. He filled his capital and country with stately buildings for his nobles ; and erected in the former a magnificent pile of buildings that might serve both for a royal residence and for public offices, a mighty and magnificent palace, richly furnished with gorgeous tapestries and variegated feather-work ; also, a lordly pile was erected for the Sovereigns of Mexico and Tlacopan. Solid materials of stone and stucco were employed in all, and they have furnished an inexhaustible quarry for the churches and other edifices since erected by the Spaniards on the site of the ancient city of Tezcuco. The time in building this latter palace is not given us, but two hundred thousand workmen, it is said, were employed on it. Nezahualcoyotl's favourite residence was at Tezcotzinco, a conical hill about two leagues from the capital. It was laid out in terraces or hanging gardens, having a flight of five hundred and twenty steps. The extraordinary accounts of Tezcucan architecture are confirmed by the relics which still cover this hill, or are half buried beneath its surface. The Tezcucan princes had but one lawful wife, though many concubines were allowed, and this great king remained unmarried to a late period. He was disappointed in an early attachment, as the princess who had been educated in privacy to be the partner of his throne gave her hand to another. The monarch submitted the affair to the proper tribunal; the parties, however, were proved to have been ignorant of the destination of the lady, and the court gave, and the monarch received, their sentence accordingly. The king diverted his chagrin by travelling. On one of his journeys he was entertained by the lord of Tepechpan, who, to do his sovereign more honour, caused him to be attended by a noble maiden, betrothed to himself. The king, who had all the amorous temperament of the South, conceived a violent passion for the lady. He kept his own counsel, and at the expense of his honour, sent an order to the chief of Tepechpan to take command of an expedition against the Tlascalans. He instructed two Tezcucan chiefs to keep near the old lord, and bring him into the thick of the fight, where he might lose his life, which, he told them, had been forfeited by a great crime, but owing to his past services he was willing to conceal his disgrace. The veteran obeyed, but in the farewell entertainment to his friends, suspecting the cause, he uttered a presentiment of his destiny, which was soon verified. The king did not think it prudent to break his passion so soon after the death of his victim, but he opened a correspondence with the princess through a female relative.

The lady was ignorant of the plot against her former fiancé's life and soon yielded to the supplications of her royal kinsman. It was arranged by him that she should appear as if for the first time, in his grounds at Tezcotzinco. The king, who was standing in a balcony of the palace, enquired who the lovely young creature was: this was followed by a public declaration of his passion, and they were soon married with great pomp, in the presence of the court and his brother monarchs.

This story, so obvious a counterpart of *David and Uriah*, is told, Prescott says, with great circumstantiality, both by the king's son and grandson, from whose narrative, the king's historian, Ixtilxochitl, derived it. They stigmatized the action as the basest of their great ancestor's life. He did not agree with his countrymen in the sanguinary rites borrowed by them from the Aztecs, but endeavoured to recall his people to the more pure and simple worship of the ancient Toltecs; but he had been married some years to his wife whom he had so unrighteously obtained, and had no issue by her. The priests said this was owing to the neglect of the gods of his country, and the only remedy was to propitiate them by human sacrifice. He gave his reluctant consent, and once more the altars smoked with the blood of slaughtered captives. But it was all in vain, and he exclaimed, "These idols of wood and stone can neither see nor feel, much less could they make the heavens and the earth, and man, the lord of it. These must be the work of the all-powerful unknown God, Creator of the universe, on whom alone I must rely for consolation and support."

He withdrew to Tezcotzinco, greatly strengthened in his former religious convictions, and openly professing his faith. To win his subjects from their degrading superstitions, he built a temple in the pyramidal form, on the summit a tower nine stories high, dedicated to *the unknown God, the Cause of causes*. It seems probable, from the emblem on the tower as well as from the complexion of his verses, that he mingled with his reverence for the Supreme the astral worship, which existed among the Toltecs. No image was allowed in the edifice, as unsuited to the "*invisible God*," and the people were prohibited from using any other sacrifice than that of the perfume of flowers and sweet scented gums. His days were chiefly spent now in the solitudes of Tezcotzinco, where he devoted himself to astronomical and, perhaps, astrological studies and meditations on his immortal destiny, and to hymns, of which the following are translations of translations :

"All the round world is but a sepulchre, and there is nothing which lives on its surface that shall not be hidden and entombed beneath it ; rivers, torrents and streams move onward to their destination, not one flows back to its present source ; they rush onward, hastening to bury themselves in the deep bosom of the ocean. The things of yesterday are no more to-day, and the things of to-day shall cease, perhaps, on the morrow. . . . But these glories have all passed away like the fearful smoke that issues from the throat of Popocatepetl. . . . The great, the wise, the valiant, the beautiful, alas ! where are they now ? They are all mingled with the clod ; and that which has befallen them shall happen to us, and to those that come after us. . . . *Then let us aspire to that heaven where all is eternal, and corruption cannot come.*" He died in the forty-third year of his reign, and the seventy-second of his age, after fitting counsel to his children and friends. "He was wise, valiant, liberal, and when we consider the magnanimity of his soul, the grandeur and success of his enterprise, his deep policy as well as his daring, we must admit him to have far surpassed every other prince and captain of this new world," says his kinsman the Tezcucan chronicler.

I should like to follow the events in his son's life, but my space is too small. He died in 1515, at the age of fifty-two, happy, Prescott says, by his timely death that he escaped seeing the fulfilment of his own predictions in the ruin of his country and the extinction of the

Indian dynasties forever. But it is clear that Montezuma, king of Mexico, by his craftiness, plundered his brother monarch of some of his most valuable domains.

If I have taken up too much space in describing what Nezahualcoyotl, the king, legislator and poet of Tezcuco, did, it has been to give the reader an adequate idea of the kind of civilization the Spaniards found in Anahuac, a civilization that was by all accounts inferior to that of the Toltecs, or, as they are sometimes called, the Nahuas, who were the first civilized and civilising natives of the country.

The Spaniards, upon their advent, found a strong government existing in Mexico, with life and property safe under it.

At its head was Montezuma, the King of the Aztecs or Mexicans, or, as he and others probably after the league spoken of had been styled, their Emperor.

The government was an elective monarchy, the sovereign being selected from the brothers of the deceased king, or in default of them, from his nephews, by four of the principal nobles chosen in the preceding reign, to whom were added the royal allies of Tezcuco and Tlacopan.

The Aztec dominion reached across the continent from the Atlantic to the Pacific. Its arms had been carried far over these limits into the farthest corner of Guatemala and Nicaragua. There were still in force the laws given by the Tezcucan king and adopted by the Aztecs; the nobles and priests were the main supporters of the national interests; the priests more indirectly, but their social influence was very great. There was great respect for morality; the security for person and property was provided for. Adultery was punishable with death; so was treason; murder—even of a slave—was a capital crime. Drunkenness in youth was a capital offence, and in persons of maturer years it was punished with much severity; but at the age of seventy it was tolerated. He who robbed in the market, or altered the measures, or removed the boundaries in the fields, was immediately put to death. The murder of a merchant or an ambassador, or any insult or injury to the latter, was considered a sufficient cause for war. The laws were represented by paintings, and the judges were attended by clever clerks or painters, who, by means of figures, described the suits of the parties concerned.

These paintings, and the hieroglyphics used by the Mexicans, have long gone out of use and understanding.

The government revenues were derived from Crown Lands set apart in the various provinces, a tax on agricultural products and a tribute on provisions and manufactured articles.

There were in their army four grades of generals, and next below them were captains. The main bodies, or regiments were eight thousand men each, and were divided into battalions of four hundred men each, and these into squads of twenty.

The Mexican skill in the science of astronomy is shown by their knowledge of the true length of the year, of the cause of eclipses, of the periods of the solstices and equinoxes.

They had public hospitals, and their physicians were skilful, but they mystified their cures with superstitious ceremonies. The merchants and military officers had a fair notion of geography; maps and charts of the country, rivers and coasts were accurately drawn, or painted on cloth. Agriculture gardening and irrigation by means of canals were far advanced. Among their chief productions were maize, cotton, cacao, the maguey, the chili, &c. The maguey, then as now, furnished the necessaries of life, and *pulque* and *mezcatl* were made from its fermented juice. From the maize they prepared sugar, from the cacao they prepared chocolate which they formed into tablets.

In mining and metallurgy they were very expert. They exercised the arts of casting, engraving, chasing and carving in metal, with great skill; and, in looms of simple construction, they made cotton cloth and other tissues, some of which were of exquisite fineness, interwoven with rabbit hair and feathers. With feathers on fine cotton webs they made garments of great magnificence. Earthenware of every description was one of the great Mexican industries, many of the articles being painted in showy colours and designs.

No beasts of burthen were used, all the carrying being done either by water or on men's backs. Despatches were carried rapidly from tower to tower, erected at intervals of six miles along the highways, where couriers were in waiting for them. Thus they were carried nearly two hundred miles in a day if needed. The women shared equally with the men as well in social festivities as in labour, but they could not inherit.

The Mexicans were simple in dress, but given to a great display of ornaments, and were courteous and polished in their manners and habits. They had no shops but barbers' shops in their towns and villages, all things being sold in the market, which, in their capital, was very large and well assorted.

They had thirteen principal deities, though they recognised a Supreme Creator and Lord of the Universe, whom they addressed in their prayers as "the invisible, incorporeal, one God of perfect perfection and purity." At the head was Huitzilopotchli, the Mexican Mars, the patron deity of the nation. A far more interesting personage in their mythology was Quetzalcoatl, the god of the air, already spoken of. He was one of those benefactors of their species who have been deified by the gratitude of posterity. No further space can be allotted to their gods, who descended in regular gradation to the *penates*, or household gods, whose little images were to be found in the humblest dwelling.

They contemplated three separate states of existence in the future: 1. The wicked were to expiate their sins in a place of everlasting darkness ; 2. Those with no other merit than having died of certain diseases were to enjoy a negative existence ; 3. Those who fell in battle, or in sac.ifice, passed at once into the highest place, into the presence of the Sun, whom they accompanied with songs and dances in his progress through the heavens.

On the death of a person his corpse was dressed in the peculiar habiliments of his tutelar deity, and strewed with pieces of paper to operate as charms against the dark road he was to travel.

A number of slaves, if he were rich, were sacrificed at his obsequies. His body was burned, and the ashes, collected in a vase, were preserved in one of the apartments of his house. "Here we have," says Prescott, " successively the usages of the Roman Catholic, the Mussulman, the Tartar, and the ancient Greek and Roman ; curious coincidences, which show how cautious we should be in adopting conclusions founded on analogy,"

In the ceremony of naming their children the infant was sprinkled with water and "the Lord was implored to permit the holy drops to wash away the sin that was given to it before the foundation of the world, so that the child might be born anew."

In more than one of their prayers they used regular forms, as, " Wilt thou blot us out, O Lord, for ever ? " " Is this punishment intended, not for our reformation, but for our destruction ?" "Impart to us, out of thy great mercy, the gifts which we are not worthy to receive through our own merits." " Keep peace with all" says another petition. " Bear injuries with humility ; God who sees, will avenge you." But the most striking parallel with Scripture that they had, is in the remarkable declaration that "he who looks too curiously on a woman, commits adultery with his eyes."

These elevated maxims were mixed up by them, with those of a puerile and even brutal character, arguing what was but the beginning of civilization.

But the priests dazzled and influenced the ignorant people, not only by their formal and pompous ceremonial, but by their astrology and divination, in which they were well initiated, and, perhaps, impressed them more than was done by the priesthood of any other country, even that of ancient Egypt.

That the sacerdotal order was numerous may be inferred from the fact that 5,000 priests were, in some way or other, attached to the principal temple of the capital.

The best instructed of this numerous body took management of the choirs ; others arranged the festivals conformably to their calendar ; some superintended the education of youth ; others had charge of hieroglyphical paintings, and oral traditions ; while the rites of sacrifice were reserved for the chief dignatries of the order. Two were at the head equal in dignity, and inferior only to the sovereign ; and the latter seldom decided any state matters of importance without their advice.

The priesthood had quarters within the precincts of their temples, and were allowed to marry. In their monastic residence they lived in stern conventual discipline, using flagellation and the thorns of the aloe to draw blood from their bodies.

The great cities were made into divisions under the charge of the clergy, and so with the towns, villages and districts, who regulated all the religious matters appertaining to them, and administered, it is worthy of remark, the rites of confession and absolution, which, however, were held to be of effect but once in a lifetime.

One of the most important duties of the priesthood was that of the education of both sexes, to which certain buildings within the enclosure of the principal temple were appropriated.

The girls were entrusted to the care of priestesses, the boys to the priests, and great attention was paid to the moral discipline of both sexes; at a suitable age for marrying, the pupils were dismissed with much ceremony.

To each of the principal temples, lands were annexed for the maintenance of the priests who managed them for themselves, and their number and value all the country over had become very great. Besides the resources from these, the religious order was enriched with first fruits, and such other offerings as were dictated, the surplus being distributed in alms.

The Mexican *teocalis* were very numerous. There were several hundred in each of the cities, and the towns, villages and districts had their share, many of them doubtless but humble edifices.

They were masses of earth cased with bricks or stone, about one hundred feet square, and in their form resembled the pyramids of Egypt, except that they were truncated.

The ascent was by four or more stories, by a flight of steps turning at angles of the pyramid, so that circuits had to be made before reaching the top, or directly to it: the top was a broad area with one or two towers forty feet or more high, in which were the images of the presiding deities, the stone of sacrifice, the altars, and the inextinguishable sacred fire. There were said to be six hundred of these altars on smaller buildings in the inclosure of the great temple of Mexico.

Human sacrifices were made of the consenting victims, those of children purchased, slaves, and mostly of prisoners of war.

They had established these sacrifices early in the fourteenth century. Prescott says, at all events, they from thenceforth became general, latterly awfully frequent; but Humboldt with his usual caution leaves it a question, whether in the antecedent period, they had not been abstemious only for want of victims, and when opportunity offered, whether they did not simply follows what was already in their minds, placed there by those from whom they descended.

The *teocali* at Mexico has been shortly described at p. 67. It stood in the midst of a vast area, encompassed by a wall of stone and lime, about eight feet high, ornamented in relief by figures of serpents, a common emblem in Anahuac as well as Egypt. The wall was quadrangular, pierced by huge battlemented gateways, opening on the four principal streets of the capital. Over each gate was a kind of arsenal, and there were barracks adjoining garrisoned by 10,000 soldiers, who were a sort of military police also. It was a pyramidal structure of earth and pebbles, and coated on the outside with the hewn stone of the country, and was in the usual form of the Aztec *teocalis*. Its circuit had a most imposing effect to the multitude in religious ceremonials. On the summit was an area paved with flat stones. The first object that met the view of Cortés, was the sacrificial stone already spoken of. At the other end of the area were two towers of three stories each, one of stone and stucco, the two upper of wood, elaborately carved. In the lower story stood the images of their gods ; the apartments above were occupied with utensils for their religious services, and the ashes of some of the Aztec princes.

Before each sanctuary stood an altar with undying fire upon it. Below were many towers and altars, and the city seemed spread out like a map, and every place was alive with business and bustle. The area of the inclosure was far more than that of the present cathedral and *plaza*. It extended into the now streets, and contained edifices for the priestesses and priests, and their pupils, granaries and other buildings. It was of itself a city within a city, and, Cortés asserted, embraced a tract of ground large enough for five hundred houses.

Such was the teocali of Mexico. It was built in the year 1486, Humboldt* says. How long it was in building is not said, probably many generations, but the Aztecs for many years used its site for their religious purposes.

I cannot tell where "Tlapallan," that the Toltecs came from was : nor where "Aztlan or Teo-Acolhucan, near Amaquemacan," that the Aztec and other tribes came from was ; though there are many theories about each, no one knows.

Yucatan now forming the States of Yucatan and Campeachy, part of Mexico, was with some of the adjacent districts of country, at the time of the arrival of the Spaniards, inhabited by the Mayas, a race of Indians. Some ethnologists say they are a distinct race ; others that

---

* This is given by Humboldt as six years before the discovery of America. That was made 12th October, 1492, as everybody knows, and so I put the year in the text 1486. The disputed point *where* the discovery was made, was set at rest by my brother, the late Rear-Admiral Becher, R.N. Assistant Hydrographer at the Admiralty, by his "Landfall of Columbus," published in 1856. He settled, from Columbus's log, that the landfall was Watling's Island, the true "Guanahani," and San Salvador, Columbus described and named. This book was borrowed by Mr. Washington Irving, and was the means of my making his charming acquaintance. He told me how he had been led into the mistake in the landfall given in his "Life of Columbus."

APPENDIX. 155

they are descended from the Toltecs ; the time of their arrival is not fixed. There are other theories, but all writers seem to agree in giving credit to the Toltecs for introducing civilisation into the peninsula. Diego de Landa, the first Bishop of Yucatan, thinks that Cuculan (the Mexican Quetzalcoatl), after much turbulence re-established order, and founded Mayapan (a name afterwards given to the whole peninsula), about the tenth century.

From Chiapas came large tribes, the Tutuxin (also Toltecs), who aided the natives to overthrow the monarch of Mayapan, about the first half of the fifteenth century. The kingdom was then divided into forty or more seignories, all doing allegiance to the *cacique* of Mani, in Yucatan. Tutul Xiu was cacique at the time of the coming of the Spaniards. See an interesting account of him and his ambassadors : 2 Stephens' Yucatan, p. 250.

Large numbers too migrated to the district of Peten. The Mayas have a language of their own which they still preserve, and Landa wrote their history, which is at the Madrid Royal Academy of History, in manuscript. The French Abbé Brasseur de Bourbourg, who knows perhaps more than any living man of this ancient people, says of it : "The alphabet and signs explained by Landa have been to me a Rosetta Stone." The calendar of the Mayas is substantially the same as the Aztecs ; Stephens says, vol. 2,120, that it shows a common origin and a similarity of worship and religious institutions between them. The hieroglyphics found at Chichen by Stephens, "beyond all question," he says, "bore the same type with those at Copan and Palenque." Their religion as to human sacrifices was, I fear, carried to even greater excess than that of the Aztecs, and their system of priesthood was much the same. In 1502, Baldwin says, the Mayas were seen by Columbus, at an island off the coast of Yucatan ; they came in "a vessel of considerable size."

The island of Cozumel, part of Yucatan, was discovered by Grijalva in 1518, following the track of Cordova, and Stephens thinks, with much reason, that, in 1841, he visited one of the ruined towers, containing a temple, that is noted in Grijalva's voyage, and that Bernal Diaz describes when Cortés visited the island a year after.

The Spaniards subdued Yucatan, though it gave them some trouble, and caused them more loss of life than all the rest of Mexico ; and the inhabitants, like the Mexicans, soon became the slaves of the invaders.

I hope I have said enough to give some idea of what the ancient people of Mexico were, on the advent of the Spaniards. Let the reader clothe and employ them according to his reading and imagination, and remember that the country was then, immensely more populous than now, was much more cultivated, and was well clothed with trees and shrubs where it is now barren. Also, that the ruins which have come to light existed when they arrived; that at all events *many of them* were then inhabited, and used by the natives ; and that the Spaniards did all they could to dismantle them, and as a rule to prevent them being inhabited or used by the natives.

Nearly all that are known stand by themselves, the houses of the native inhabitants having disappeared, and are imbedded in trees. In, upon and about them are growths of large forest trees; and it has been matter of regret to me, that, in the instance of Copan and Palenque, the explorers who cut down trees in and about the ruins, did not take the trouble to count the rings they bore. They would have given them an approximation, at all events, to the number of years they had been deserted by man.

Not only does a tree tell its age by the number of rings, each indicating a year's growth, but it can be made to tell the date of marks upon it.

Suppose a surveyors' line was made fifty years or so ago, evidenced by his making the usual *blazes* (striking off with the axe a strip of wood and bark from every few trees along his line), and that the trees are still standing. The wound is healed and there is a healthy bark over each blaze; but a practised surveyor detects a slightly raised ridge in the bark, cuts down where it exists to the blackened surface the axe has left, fifty or more years before, and counting the rings that have grown between that and the bark, finds about the number of years since the blaze has been made. The field notes of the original surveyor, and other things concurring, this evidence is, in the Ontario Superior Courts, considered conclusive.

I have been counsel in many cases where such evidence was offered; in one case I remember the *blazes* were some 70 years old. No man can create this evidence, and nature and the trees are not to be contradicted.

But it is time to go to the ruins this paper is written about.

TULA.

The Toltecs arrived here in 670, the Aztecs in 1196, Humboldt states. It is situated about 30 miles from the City of Mexico, in the State of Hidalgo, on the banks of the river Tula or Montezuma, which joins the river Tampico, near its mouth in the Gulf of Mexico.

Prescott (p. 4) says: "The Toltecs established their capital at Tula, north of the Mexican valley, and the remains of extensive buildings were to be discovered there at the time of the conquest."

THE PYRAMIDS OF SAN JUAN TEOTIHUACAN.

These are referred to in letter No. 3. See pages 43 to 47 and notes.

Humboldt speaks of them as "the most ancient of all;" he adds that Siguenza believed them to be the work of the Olmecs, and that the Toltecs "appear to have constructed the pyramid of Cholula on their model."

THE PYRAMID OF CHOLULA AS IT IS.
(From a photo, by Messrs. Kilburn Brothers.)

The Abbé Brasseur de Bourbourg, p. 64, states, "that the first human sacrifices of the Mexicans were offered here."

THE PYRAMID OF CHOLULA.

See description ante, pages 100, 101 and note.

I must add that the brick which most resisted my stick, was there called "burned;" and that as will be seen, a heap, I remember calling my party's attention to as a "baby pyramid," was part of the original, cut off from it.

Here is a photo as it is, from one by Messrs. Kilburn Brothers, and on the opposite page is a photo from a drawing of Humboldt's, as he saw its west side, about the year 1803.

Upon the coming of the Aztecs, with the other six tribes mentioned to Mexico, they found the pyramids of Teotihuacan, this pyramid and that of Papantla, and they attributed the building of all to the Toltecs; but it is possible that they were constructed before even their arrival, that is before 648. "We are not to be surprised" says Humboldt, "that the history of the American people begins before the seventh century, and that that of the Toltecs is uncertain. A profound *savant* gives evidence to prove that the history of the north of Europe goes only back to the tenth century, when the plateau of Mexico offered a more advanced civilization than Denmark, Sweden and Russia."

He says that in cutting the new road from Puebla to Mexico, on the side opposite Popocatapetl, and on the north side where the first tier or story is traversed by the road, a large portion of the pyramid is cut through and detached. This detached mass is one-eighth of the original, and he discovered that it was built of alternate layers of clay and brick, which latter are generally eight centimetres high by forty long. It appeared to him they were not baked, but merely dried in the sun; but they may have been submitted to a slight firing, and it may be that the layers of clay are not in the interior of the pyramid, separating the bricks. It has four tiers of equal height, intended to face the cardinal points, but that, from the edges of the tiers not being very distinct, it was hard to recognize their original direction. The base, he said, was more extended than that of any like monument on the old continent. His measurements are, height 54 metres, each side of the base 439 metres.

He says that Bernal Diaz, a soldier of Cortés army counted the steps of the teocalis; in that of Mexico, he made 140; in that of Tezcuco, 117; and in that of Cholula, 120. In cutting off the detached mass above mentioned, a square chamber was discovered, built of stone and sustained by beams of cypress. In it were two skeletons, some idols in basalt, and a great number of vases glazed and painted with art. These were not preserved, but Humboldt was assured that this chamber, which was covered with brick and clay had no outlet.

He noticed a disposition of the bricks tending to diminish the pressure of the roof; that very large bricks were placed horizontally, in such a manner that those above overlapped the under ones, and the result was a mass in grades or steps which supplied in a measure the Gothic arch. He mentions many traditions concerning this monument and the temple to Quetzalcoatl, found on it by the Spaniards, and the substitution of a small chapel by them on it, dedicated to our Lady of the Remedies. Among the traditions of the Indians, was one that the gods, jealous that this edifice would reach the clouds, threw fire from heaven upon it, and that the work was stopped, many workmen having perished. Afterwards it was dedicated to Quetzalcoatl.

Humboldt was reminded strongly by these and other Mexican monuments of the Temple of Belus, as described by Herodotus, whose measurement and description he gives.

He also gives the relation of Diodorus, that the Babylonian temple served as an observatory of the stars by the Chaldeans, "the rising and setting of which could be accurately discerned, on account of the great height of the building."

The Mexican priests also observed the position of the stars from the top of this and other teocalis, and announced to the people the hours of the night by blowing a horn.

He adds, that these teocalis were built between the years 571 and 1416, and that one cannot see without surprise, that these American edifices of which the form is almost identical with that of the oldest monuments on the shores of the Euphrates, belong to times so near our own.

Since Humboldt wrote, much research and many excavations have been made in and about ancient Babylon. Layard in his "discoveries among the ruins of Ninevah and Babylon," p. 422, says: "The Birs Nimrond (the palace of Nimrod) of the Arabs, and 'the prison of Nebuchadnezzar' of the Jews, are by old travellers believed to be the very ruins of the tower of Babel; by some again supposed to represent the temple of Belus, the wonder of the ancient world; and by others the site of Borsippa, a city celebrated as the high place of the Chaldean worship, is a vast heap of bricks, clay and broken pottery. It rises to the height of 198 feet, and has on its summit a compact mass of brick work 37 feet high by 28 broad. * * * It is pierced by square holes, apparently made to admit air through the compact structure."

Sir Austin adds, at p. 426—"Without, however, venturing to identify the Birs Nimroud with the ruins of this temple, it may be observed, that it is highly probable one uniform system of building was adopted in the East for sacred purposes, and that these ascending and receding platforms formed the general type of the Chaldean and Assyrian temples. A step may still be traced around the foot of the ruin, probably part of the basement or first platform, and the whole is surmounted by the remains of a quadrangular enclosure; it is in every respect like those in the Desert to the West of Mosul."

APPENDIX.

A very recent traveller, Grattan Geary, in his book, "Through Asiatic Turkey," just published, says—"For several centuries, the Birs Nimroud enjoyed the reputation of being the remains of the Tower of Babel, but the modern archæologists are inclined to believe that it was the famous temple of Belus, restored or enlarged by Nebuchadnezzar, whose name is on many of the bricks of which it is built. * * * It looks like a natural hill, but it was built up stage by stage, there being eight in all, each of those above the first being smaller than that on which it rested." Then, speaking of the brick work on the summit, he says—"Holes like unto pigeon-holes, go through it from side to side. What purpose they were intended to serve, no one can even guess."

In the "American Cyclopedia" title "Babel," I find the following: "The general description given by Herodotus tallies so clearly with the mound of Birs Nimroud, as to render it probable that this is the remains of the temple of Belus.

"The ruin presents the aspect of a large irregular mound, rising abruptly from a wide desert plain with masses of vitrified matter lying around its base; its interior is found, upon excavation, to be composed of a mass of bricks, partially vitrified by fire, shewing that it is the ruin of a structure into which combustible material largely entered."

The monuments and mounds that Humboldt refers to, as existing on the shores of the Euphrates, are almost countless.

PAPANTLA

Is a village of the State of Vera Cruz, distant about 60 miles north-east of Jalapa, and about 25 from Tuxpan.

In a thick forest near this village rises the pyramid of Papantla, which Humboldt visited about 1803. It was discovered he says, about 1773, by some Spanish huntsmen, and is described by him as a steeper teocali than any other of the kind, with six or perhaps seven stages or stories. The height of it he gives as nearly eighteen metres, while the length of the base is only twenty. This little edifice is built entirely of free stone of extraordinary size, beautifully and regularly cut, and three stair-cases lead to the summit. The exterior is adorned with sculptures, hieroglyphics, and small niches are disposed with much symmetry; these niches appear to have reference to the signs of the calendar of the Toltecs. There seems to be no later description of this monument published than Humboldt's, and it would well repay the explorer for a visit.

XOCHICALCO.

This is the last monument appearing in this paper that Humboldt visited in person. It is about fifteen miles from the Town of Cuernavaca, south of the City of Mexico, on the western slope of the Cordilleras. It rises, he says, on an isolated hill 117 metres high from the base, and is called Xochicalco, or the house of flowers. It is a mass of rock to which the hand of man has given a tolerably regular conical form, and is divided into five tiers or terraces, each of which is covered with masonry. The tiers have nearly twenty metres of perpendicular elevation, receding towards the summit, like the Aztec pyramids. All the terraces incline towards the south-east, probably to facilitate the flow of rain-water which is very abundant in this region.

The hill is surrounded by a rather deep and very large moat, so that the whole intrenchment is nearly four thousand metres in circumference. The summit of the hill presents an oblong platform, which from north to south is seventy-two metres broad, and from east to west eighty-six metres long. This platform is surrounded by a wall of free stone, the height of which exceeds two metres, and which was intended as a defence. In the centre of this spacious Place d'Armes are the remains of a pyramidal monument which had five tiers, the first of which only has been preserved. The proprietors of a neighbouring sugar mill, were barbarous enough to destroy the pyramid and carry off the stones to build their ovens. The Indians declare that the five tiers were still in existence in 1750, and according to the dimensions of the first, it may be supposed that the whole edifice was twenty metres high. The tiers are placed exactly according to the four cardinal points. The base is 20 M. ·7 long by 17 M. ·4 wide. No vestige of a staircase has been discovered—a very striking circumstance, as it is asserted that there was formerly on the top a stone seat covered with hieroglyphics.

Travellers who have examined this work of the aborigines of America could not sufficiently admire the polish and cut of the stones, which are all "parallelopipeds," the care with which they are united without cement, and the execution of the carvings with which the tiers are adorned; each figure occupies several stones at once, and the outline not being interrupted by the joints of the stones, it is supposed that the reliefs were sculptured after the edifice was built. Amongst the hieroglyphical ornaments are heads of crocodiles, which throw out water, and figures of men seated with crossed legs, like the Asiatics.

The fosse surrounding the hill, the coating of the tiers, the great number of subterranean apartments cut in the rock on the north side, the wall which defends the approach to the platform, all concur to give to Xochicalco the character of a military monument.

The great resemblance between it and the Aztec teocalis inclined Humboldt to the belief that it was nothing but a fortified temple. The pyramid or great temple of Tenochtitlan, also enclosed an arsenal, and served during the siege as a stronghold—sometimes to the Mexicans, and sometimes to the Spaniards.

This monument is attributed to the Toltecs; everything that is lost in obscurity is attributed to the people who are supposed to have possessed the genius of civilization. Abridged from p. 129, vol. 1.

MIZANTLA.

A ruined city in the State of Vera Cruz, Mexico, thirty-five miles north-east of Jalapa. Its remains comprise a pyramid, streets, ancient walls, &c., and see ante pages 131, and the letter of the United States Consul, at page 134 n. as to the other half of the Aztec Calendar stone discovered there by Senor M. Melgar, of the City of Vera Cruz.

Baldwin says, p. 91, "It is known that important ruins exist in the forests of Papantla and Mizantla, which have never been described."

MITLA

Is a village of the State of Oxaca, 26 miles east from the City of Oxaca, and gives its name to the ruins. Humboldt says of them that originally there existed five separate buildings disposed with great regularity. A very large gate, of which there were still (his book from which I quote is published in 1816) some vestiges, led to a spacious court fifty metres square. Heaps of earth and remains of subterranean structures indicated that four edifices surrounded this court; and in the principal edifice, known as the palace, was distinguished, a terrace raised one or two metres above the level of the court and surrounding the wall, and a niche formed in the wall, a metre and a half above the level of the *hall with pillars*. This niche, which is broader than it is high, he says, no doubt enclosed an idol.

The principal door of the hall was covered with a stone.

An entrance of the inner court; a well or opening of the tomb were distinguished, as also, a very broad staircase which led to an excavation in the form of a cross, supported by columns. The two galleries intersecting at right angles, were each 27 metres long and 8 broad. The walls were covered with *Grecques* and Arabesques.

There were also six columns intended to support the beams of savin wood that formed the ceiling, three of which were then in good preservation. The roof consisted of very large slabs, and the columns which indicated the infancy of art, were the *only ones then found*, and were without capitals. They were monoliths, and were 5 metres ·8 high. There were a number of apartments, in the interior of which were paintings representing weapons, trophies and sacrifices. He speaks of the mosaic, which he says is composed of small square stones, which are placed with much skill by the side of each other on a mass of clay, which appears to fill up the inside of the wall, and notices that the different parts of the palace present very striking irregularities or want of symmetry. As to the Greek ornaments, he says they offer, no doubt, striking analogy with those of Lower Italy, but, as he has already observed, that analogies of this kind are very limited proof of ancient communications of nations.

In the environs of Mitla are the remains of a great pyramid, and some other buildings resembling those he has described; he adds, that Mitla is a contraction of the word Miguitlan, which means in the Mexican language—*place of desolation, place of woe.*

Baldwin says of them, p. 121, quoting M. Charnay, "that their beauty can be matched only by the monuments of Greece and Rome, in their best days." Speaking of one of the buildings, he adds: "It is a bewildering maze of courts and buildings, with facings ornamented with mosaics in relief, of the purest design; but under its projections are found traces of paintings, wholly primitive in style, in which the right line is not even respected. These rude designs, associated with palaces so correct in architecture, and so ornamented with panels of mosaic of such marvellous workmanship, put strange thoughts in the mind. Must we not suppose these palaces were occupied by a race less advanced in civilization than their first builders?"

Baldwin further says that "Two miles or more away from the great edifices here mentioned towards the west, is the "Castle of Mitla." It was built on the summit of an isolated and precipitous wall of rock, which is accessible only on its east side. The whole levelled summit of this hill is enclosed by a solid wall of hewn stone twenty-one feet thick and eighteen high. This wall has salient and retiring angles, with curtains interspersed. On its east side it is flanked by double walls. Within the enclosure are the remains of several small buildings. The field of these ruins was very large three hundred years ago; at that time it may have included this castle."—*Ancient America*, p. 122.

The palace of Mitla was built by the Tzapotecs, anciently inhabiting Oxaca. Humboldt says, and according to traditions which he collects, the principal purpose of it, and the buildings close by, was to mark the spot where the ashes of their princes reposed.

The Tzapotecs, as has been already observed, were among the most ancient nations of Mexico.

And be it remembered here that whenever a metre is spoken of by Humboldt, he means, according to the Imperial Dictionary, *thirty-nine inches and thirty-seven hundredths of an inch.*

PALENQUE

Is a village in the State of Chiapas, Mexico, 100 miles E. N.E. of Ciudad Real, and gives its name to the ruins, which are about seven miles distant from it.

They were discovered in 1750 by some Spaniards in travelling, who said they covered from eighteen to twenty-four miles.

APPENDIX. 163

In 1787, Captain Antonio del Rio was commissioned by the King of Spain to explore them; he complained of the thickness of the forest then. His report slept, so far as England and the United States are concerned, till 1822.

While this report slept in the archives of Guatemala, Charles the 4th, of Spain, commissioned Captain Dupaix to make further explorations.

By various accidents, what Dupaix saw and did was not given to the public till 1825, when his work was published in Paris at 800 francs a copy; Lord Kingborough's, so far as regards Palenque is a mere repetition of Dupaix, was $400 a copy.

John Lloyd Stephens, the great American traveller and writer, born in Shrewsbury, New Jersey, in 1805, died in 1852, has done more than any man living or dead to explore and give to the public an idea of what these Central American ruins were, was at Palenque with Mr. Catherwood as draughtsman, in 1840, and he wrote "Incidents of Travel in Central America, Chiapas, and Yucatan," publishing it through Harper Brothers, in 1841. M. DeWaldeck had, while Stephens was at Palenque, already passed more than two years there, and subsequently with the French Abbé and historian, Brasseur de Bourbourg (well known in Lower Canada as the author of "Histoire du Canada," 2 vols. Quebec, 1852), passed some time there.

The result of their labours "Monuments anciens du Mexique, et autres ruines de l'ancienne civilisation du Mexique," the designs by DeWaldeck, the text by Brasseur de Bourbourg, was published in Paris in 1866.

This learned writer was much in Mexico, and has written much about it and the people of America as they were before Columbus's discovery of it.

The ruins are in a large forest, and all the explorers had to cut down numbers of trees growing in and about the ruins, to enable them to see, or depict anything.

The discoveries brought to light are as follows:—

A building, which is called, as other like large ruined buildings are, the "palace," and stands with its face to the east. It is 228 feet in front, by 180 deep. The height 25 feet, with a projecting cornice, all of stone: the front contains fourteen doorways, about nine feet wide each, and the intersecting piers are between six and seven feet wide. On the left, as you approach, eight of the piers have fallen down, as has also the right-hand corner: the terrace underneath is cumbered with ruins. But six piers remain entire, and the rest of the front was, at the time of Stephens' visit, open.

The front view of this building shews it was surmounted with a tower, whose base was thirty feet square; it had three stories, and was conspicuous by its height and proportions.

Within this tower was found another, distinct from the outer one.

The interior of the palace is taken up with courts, corridors, and chambers, with ranges of steps and grand staircases, court-yards with grim gigantic figures, nine or more feet high, carved in stone, in *bas relief*, a plan of which, Stephens gives and which are well worthy of such an enormous building.

The tower and palace are substantially built of stone, with a mortar of lime and sand, and the whole front was covered with stucco and painted.

The piers were ornamented with spirited *bas reliefs*, and there were hieroglyphics and richly ornamented borders on them, the colours found on them being red, blue, and yellow.

The palace stands on an elevation of an oblong form, 40 feet high, 310 feet in front and rear, and 260 feet on each side. This was faced with stone, and was probably in steps; but the stones have been thrown down by the growth of trees, and its form was then, when Stephens visited it, hardly distinguishable. Brasseur de Bourbourg gives the height of the pyramid on which the palace stands, as sixty feet, however. At the south-west corner of the palace is a ruined pyramidal structure, on the truncated top of which is, what Mr. Stephens gives as No. 1, of what the Indians call the "casas, or houses of Piedra." It is 76 feet in front and 25 feet deep. It had, he says, five doors and six piers all standing, and all the front was richly ornamented in stucco, and covered with hieroglyphics, four of the piers having human figures in *bas relief* in stucco.

The interior of this building is divided into two corridors, with its ceiling, like that of the palace, nearly a point, from the peculiar form of arch of the building; something like an isosceles triangle with its upper angle cut off by the finish given, of a stone across its top.

In the corridor are three tablets of hieroglyphics well preserved, which Stephens says, are the same in character that were found by him at Copan and Quirigua.

Stephens was the first to give them to the public, and he says that both Captains Del Rio and Dupaix refer to them, but in few words, and neither gives any drawing of them.

He adds there was no staircase or means of communication between the tower and upper part of this building.

In front of it, at the foot of the pyramidal structure, was a small stream, and the remains of an old stone aqueduct, from which it was supplied. Crossing this stream he found a broken stone terrace about 60 feet on the slope, with a level esplanade at the top 110 feet broad, from which rose another pyramidal structure, ruined, and overgrown with trees, 134 feet high, on the slope, and at its summit is what he calls No. 2 casa, 30 feet front, 31 feet deep, and having three doorways. The whole front was covered with stuccoed ornaments, and the two outer piers contained hieroglyphics.

In the interior, were two corridors and ceilings as before, and the pavement of large square stones. The back corridor is divided into three apartments, with heavy mouldings of stucco and cornice ; on each side of the doorway there had been a sculptured stone ; and within is a chamber where there is no admission of light except from the door ; on its back wall, was the tablet, two-thirds of which are given in his engraving. It was then 10 feet 8 inches wide, 6 feet 4 inches in height, and consisted of three separate stones.

That on the left, facing the spectator is still in its place ; the middle one had been removed and was carried down the stream ; it was there copied, and is given in its original position in the wall. The stone on the right is broken and gone, but probably contains, like the one on the left, hieroglyphics.

This is the famous *tablet of the cross*, and the principal subject is the cross. It is surmounted by a strange bird, and there are two human figures right and left of it, who are evidently important personages — their costume is in a style that seems new, and is of a soft and pliable texture.

Both are looking towards the cross, and one seems in the act of making an offering to it, perhaps of a child.

There are hieroglyphics about it, which doubtless explain all Stephens says, and reminded him of the Egyptian mode of recording the name, history, &c., of the persons represented.

On account of this cross, Dupaix and his commentators assumed for this building a very remote antiquity, in a period at all events antecedent to the Christian era ; accounting for the appearance of the cross, by the argument that it was known, and had a symbolical meaning among ancient nations, long before it became the emblem of the Christian faith.

From the foot of the elevation in which stands the last building, their bases almost touching, rises another pyramidal structure like the last, in which was the house he called casa No. 3, which was 38 feet in front by 28 feet deep. It was ornamented in stucco, and had piers and an interior something like the last, in which as in this he found an enclosed chamber, both of which he called adoratories, or altars.

Within this casa No. 3 the chamber was four feet seven inches deep and nine feet wide, and set in the back of its wall was a stone tablet nine feet long by eight feet high, a copy of which he gives. Like the other with the cross it is composed of three separate stones ; the sculpture was perfect; the two human figures are the same as those represented in the tablet of the cross. Both stand on the backs of human beings, one of whom supports himself by his hands and knees, the other seeming crushed by the weight. In the centre is a mask which Stephens thought afterwards was similar or had a likeness to the one Humboldt shewed in his book of the Aztec Stone ; and this was one of the reasons for the conclusion he came to about the people who built these monuments. The piers on each side of the doorway to this tablet, contained each a stone tablet with figures carved in bas relief, which he gives in his book at p. 353, and there is also a drawing of the chamber in casa No. 3, which I have partly described from him.

He says of this, "We could not but regard it as a holy place, dedicated to the gods, and consecrated by the religious observances of a lost and unknown people. To us it was all a mystery; silent, defying the most scrutinizing gaze, and reach of intellect."

Near to this on the top of another pyramidal structure, was another building, but so ruined and shattered, apparently by an earthquake, that it was impossible even to make out the ground plan.

Then returning to the Casa No. 1, and proceeding south about 1500 feet, on another pyramidal structure, was another building, marked in his plan No. 4, which was 20 feet front and 18 feet deep, but very ruinous in condition. Fronting the door and against the back wall of the inner corridor, was a large stucco ornament representing a figure sitting on a couch, but a great part had been taken off and carried away. The body of the couch, with tiger's feet, is all that there remained. The outline of two tigers' heads and of the sitting personage, was seen in the wall.

It seems to have been superior in execution to any other stucco relief in Palenque. The body of the couch he says was entire, and the leg and foot hanging down the side are "elegant specimens of art and models for study." M. De Waldeck makes his plate 42 of this, restored.

There were no doors, or remains of any, of any kind. Within, on each side, were three niches in the wall, eight or ten inches square, with a cylindrical stone about two inches in diameter fixed upright, by which, perhaps, a door was secured.

Along the cornice outside, about a foot from the front, holes were drilled, at intervals, through the stone; and his impression was, that an immense cotton cloth was raised and lowered by their means. Such a custom, he says, was, at the time he wrote, used in front of the piazzas of some haciendas in Yucatan.

There were no beams or lintels found over the doors, or rather doorways, of any kind or description, and the stone above on each was broken somewhat. Stephens inferred, the lintels had been of wood, which had decayed and disappeared.

The separating walls of the palace, like many other of the walls of buildings he describes, had apertures of about a foot, he thought for ventilation. Some of them were of the forms which have been called the Greek Cross and the Egyptian Tau, he adds; and made the subject of much learned speculation. Such is the substance of what Stephens says he found. He adds that, considering the space occupied by the ruins, and supposing the houses of the inhabitants, like those of the Egyptians and the present race of Indians.

THE TOWER OF THE PALACE, PALENQUE.
(*From a drawing of M. De Waldeck.*)

were of frail and perishable materials, and, as at Memphis and Thebes, to have disappeared altogether, the city may have covered an immense extent; and thus he concludes:

"Here were the remains of a cultivated, polished, and peculiar people. * * We lived in the ruined palaces of their kings, we went up to their desolate temples and fallen altars; and wherever we moved we saw the evidences of their taste, their skill in arts, their wealth and pains. We fancied every building perfect, with its terraces and pyramids, its sculptured and painted ornaments, grand, lofty and imposing, &c."

Except in the height of the pyramid, on which stands the palace, the two explorers agree substantially enough for this paper. Each gives an engraving of a bas relief in stucco, on the west side of the palace—it is No. 2 in plate 13 of Brasseur de Bourbourg's book, and he makes mention of it; I think the other does not, and it is found much inferior to the other, at the back of p. 317 of his book.

Both these engravings show as part of the headdress of the standing figure in the bas relief, an *elephant's head and trunk*.

Where did the builders get this?

Brasseur de Bourbourg thinks the architecture of the tower admirable, and that one man only was intended to defend it.

I copy here his plate of the tower, or rather M. De Waldeck's, which shows some of the bas reliefs in the piers, and roots of trees going downwards, outside the tower in search of nourishment.

From each of the buildings Stephens found, none of the others were to be seen; and without a guide they might have gone within a hundred feet of them, he says, so thick was the forest.

Captain Caddy, R.A., who Stephens mentions was there shortly before him, told me that in walking about Palenque, for miles it seemed to him, he was treading on the *debris* of old stone buildings.

But the space examined by the explorer has been but small. Stephens says, once only he attempted an exploration.

From the door of the palace, almost in a line with its front, rose a high, steep mountain, which he thought must command a view of the ruins, and, perhaps, itself contain ruins.

He took its bearing, and, with compass in hand and an Indian before him with his machete, cut a straight line E.N.E. to its top. It was so steep he had to haul himself up by branches, and on the top was a high mound of stones, with a foundation wall, still remaining. Trees were growing out of the top, up one of which he climbed, but could not see the palace or any of the buildings. Behind, nothing was to be seen but forest; in front, only a wooded plain extending to Tobasco and the Gulf of Mexico.

At ten leagues distance is the village of Las Tres Cruces, or the Three Crosses, which Cortés erected there in his march from the City of Mexico to Honduras.

Mr. Stephens supposes Palenque was then desolate and in ruins, or Cortés would have turned aside to subdue and plunder it; Brasseur de Bourbourg, on the contrary, thinks it was a prosperous place at the time of the Spanish Conquest, whatever name it then bore. See p. 82.

OCOSINGO

Is a town in the State of Chiapas, Mexico, sixty-five miles south-east of Ciudad Real.

Captain Dupaix was here in 1807; but whether he says anything about the ruins I do not know. They are about eight miles from the town, and were visited by Mr. Stephens, in 1840.

He found a high structure, probably a fortress, he says, rising in a pyramidal form, with fine spacious terraces, which had all been faced with stone, but were broken and overgrown. On the top was a pyramidal structure, overgrown with trees, supporting a building. This was fifty feet in front, thirty-five feet in depth, well built of stone and lime, and was once covered with stucco, part of which and the cornice remained.

The entrance was by a doorway ten feet wide, which led into an ante-chamber leading into another chamber, ten feet square. The roof was of stone, lapped over in the usual style of the arch, as made by the architects of the new world. There were several chambers, but it was much ruined and choked with debris when he wrote. Over the main door was an ornament of stucco, which at first impressed him by its striking resemblance to the winged globe, over the doors of Egyptian temples. It was much broken, but the part that remained in its place is represented in his engraving at p. 259, and differs in detail from the winged globe. The wings were reversed, there was a fragment of circular ornament which may have been intended for a globe, but there were no remains of serpents entwining on it. Over this, the door lintel was a *beam of wood*, quite sound; and both he and Mr. Catherwood were satisfied it had been trimmed with an instrument of metal.

There was a subterranean apartment with curious stucco ornaments. They saw another edifice on a still higher structure, and then two others, each on pyramidal elevations; but all were much ruined. They then came out on the table-land, the probable site of the old city which was protected on all sides by the same high terraces. These ruins were but hurriedly visited by Stephens. He is inclined to think, as Brasseur de Bourbourg does, that they were those of an inhabited city, at the time of the conquest by the Spaniards.

UXMAL.

The ruins take their name, like most of the others, from an adjoining hacienda, that of Uxmal. They are in the peninsula of Yucatan, in the

State of Campeachy, Mexico, and are distant from Merida, the chief city of Yucatan, which contains more than 30,000 inhabitants, and is about 20 miles from Progresso, and the same distance from Sisal, its ports, sixty-nine miles.

Stephens, of whom I have already spoken, was at these ruins in 1840, and again in the latter part of 1841. His book is principally quoted from.*

On his first visit the ground in and about these ruins had been cleared; but on the second the growth of underbrush and cane was ten and more feet high, which he had to remove to inspect and measure and get sketched these buildings as he has done.

The buildings are in a very large space, and no doubt, with the debris found, mark the site of a large ancient city. They are the house or palace of the governor, the house of the dwarf, the house or palace of the nuns, the house of the old woman, the house of the tortoises, and the house of the pigeons, all built of stone on platforms and elevations; and there are mounds and elevations having no name, and boundary walls in a more or less state of ruin; and here let me add, that the names given to these buildings are modern and arbitrary, and such as they are known by among all the people belonging to the hacienda. The buildings are very imposing in appearance in their present condition, and the following are Stephens' measurements and description.

THE HOUSE OR PALACE OF THE GOVERNOR, UXMAL,

Stands on three great terraces; the front is towards the east and 322 feet; the ends are 39 feet wide; in what he calls the centre doorway is a very large and elaborate sculptured ornament of stone. Up to the cornice and on all four of its sides the facade presents a smooth surface, and above is one solid mass of rich complicated and elaborately sculptured ornaments, forming a sort of arabesque. Each of these ornaments is made up of separate stones, each of which had carved on it part of the subject, and was then set in its place in the wall. It may be called a sort of sculptured mosaic; and he has no doubt that each stone is part of a history, allegory, or fable. The roof is flat and had been covered with cement; and the rear was a solid wall without openings nine feet in thickness. Like the front, it was ornamented with sculptured stone. It has eleven doorways in front, and one at each end; the doors were all gone, and what had been wooden lintels over them had fallen; but in other buildings many of the wooden lintels were left.

The interior was divided longitudinally by a wall into two corridors, and these again into oblong rooms, by cross partitions. Every pair of these rooms communicated by a doorway opposite that in front. The principal apartments in the centre were sixty feet long and twenty-

---

* Stephens' "Incidents of Travels in Yucatan." Harper & Bros.: New York.

three feet high to the top of the arch. The walls were of square, smooth blocks of stone, and the floors were of cement, in some places broken and crumbling. The ceiling was a triangular arch, as at Palenque, without the key-stone. The support is made by stones overlapping and presenting a smooth surface to within about a foot of the point of meeting, and there covered by a layer of flat stones. Here and there, were two conspicuous marks, which were found afterwards in all the ruined buildings of the country. They were the prints of a *red hand*, with the thumb and fingers extended. He who had made it had pressed his hand moistened with red paint against the stone.

The three terraces, on top of which is the palace of the governor, at Uxmal, are hardly less imposing than itself. The lowest is 3 feet high, 15 feet broad, and 575 feet long; the second 20 feet high, 250 feet wide, and 540 feet long; and the third, on which the building stands, is 19 feet high, 30 feet broad, and 360 feet in front. They were all supported by substantial stone walls; that of the second was in a good state of preservation; all the corners of these platforms were rounded, instead of presenting sharp angles. Stephens speaks of an oblong structure along the south end on the second platform, about 3 feet high, 200 feet long, and 15 feet wide; at the foot of which there is a range of pedestals, and fragments of columns, and of large rudely sculptured stone, carved with two heads, buried. This was done, he suggests, by the Spaniards, when they drove out the inhabitants and depopulated the city, following their example at Cholula, and elsewhere, in throwing down and burying idols.

On the second great platform, a grand staircase, 130 feet broad, which once contained thirty-five steps, rises and leads to the third platform, on which the building stands. Beside this staircase there is nothing leading to it; and the only other approach to the second platform is by an inclined plane 100 feet broad, at the south end of the building.

One of the photographs, mentioned at p. 132 ante, is of this palace of the governor, and is copied herewith made very small, requiring the use of a magnifying-glass to see its mosaic work.

A NAMELESS MOUND, UXMAL.

On a line with the back of the palace of the governor, is a very high, large, but nameless mound, its sides encased with stone, and in many parts richly ornamented. It is 65 feet high, and 300 feet wide on one of its bases, 200 on the other. On the top was a platform of stone, 75 feet square, with a border of sculptured stone.

THE HOUSE OF THE DWARF, UXMAL.

The court-yard of this building is 135 feet by 85, and is bounded by ranges of mounds from 25 to 30 feet thick, covered with a rank growth

of herbage, but which, perhaps, formed ranges of buildings. The pyramid and elevation on which the House of the Dwarf stands, is very steep, of stone, and in parts much ruined. It is 235 feet long, by 155 wide; its height 85 feet; its ends are rounded; and from the ground to the top of the building is 105 feet. At the height of 60 feet from the ground is a projecting platform, on which is a building loaded with ornaments.

No communication with this building remained, but Stephens thought he detected the ruins of a triangular arch, which supported a grand staircase, once leading to the door of this building.

The crowning structure, the House of the Dwarf, is a long narrow building 72 feet by 12, and is much ruined; but is tastefully decorated, more so, Stephens thought, than the others. The interior is divided into three apartments; that in the centre being 24 feet by 7, and those on each side 19 by 7.

A narrow platform, 5 feet wide, projects from the four sides of this building; and to its eastern front ascends a grand staircase 102 feet high, 70 feet wide, and containing 90 steps.

THE HOUSE, OR PALACE OF THE NUNS, UXMAL,

Is a quadrangular building, with a court-yard in the centre, standing on the last of three terraces, nineteen feet high. The front of this building is 79 feet, and above the cornice, from one end to the other, it is ornamented with sculpture. In the centre is a large gateway, spanned by the triangular arch, and leading to the courtyard; and on each side of the gateway are four doorways opening to apartments, averaging 24 feet long, 10 wide, and 17 feet high to the top of the arch. The building forming the right side of this quadrangle is 158 feet long; that on the left 173 feet: and at the end, or range opposite the front it measures 264 feet. These three ranges are all dead walls on the exterior, and above, the cornice is all ornamented with the same rich sculpture.

Passing through the gateway, a court-yard is entered, with four great façades looking down upon it, each ornamented from one end to the other with rich and intricate carving, surpassing all that is to be seen among these ruins. This yard is 214 by 258 feet.

One of the ornaments here is the figure of a human being much mutilated; and the bodies of the many serpents represented in the sculpture are covered with feathers.

At the end of this court-yard, fronting the entrance-gate, appears a lofty building, 264 feet long, on a terrace 20 feet high. The ascent is by a grand but ruined staircase, 95 feet wide; and on each side is a building with a sculptured front and having doorways leading to appartments. Within all is crowded with elaborate sculpture.

The building is erected *over, and completely incloses*, a smaller one of older date but much like it. As to the sculpture facing this court-yard, on the House of the Nuns, it would be difficult to have more variety and, at the same time, more harmony of ornament. The apartments opening upon this yard were 88 in number.

One of the photographs mentioned at page 132 is of about one-fourth of the front of this Palace of the Nuns, and is copied and herewith, made very small, requiring the use of a magnifying glass to see its mosaic work.

THE HOUSE OF THE OLD WOMAN, UXMAL,

Is much ruined. It is about 500 feet from the Palace of the Governor, and takes its name from a mutilated statue of an old woman lying before it. It is only remarkable as one of these ancient structures.

THE HOUSE OF TORTOISES, UXMAL,

Is so called from a bead, or row, of tortoises in stone which goes round its cornice, is 94 feet in front and 34 feet deep. It stands alone, and wants the rich and gorgeous decorations of the palace of the governor, on the second terrace or elevation of which it is built. It is of remarkable beauty in its proportions, and the chasteness of its ornaments. Although standing on the second platform of the palace of the governor it has no visible communication with it, and will soon be a mass of ruins.

THE HOUSE OF THE PIGEONS, UXMAL,

Is 240 feet long; and along the centre of the roof, running longitudinally, is a range of structures built in a pyramidal form nine in number, about 3 feet thick, with small oblong openings through them, which give them, somewhat, the appearance of pigeon houses; hence the name. All have been covered with ornaments, some of which still remain. It has an arch-way and a court-yard: at the end of this is a range of ruined buildings, with another arch-way in the centre. Passing through this archway another large court-yard is reached, on either side of which is a range of ruined buildings; and at the farther end is a great teocali. A broad stair-case leads to the top of this, on which stands a long narrow building, 100 feet by 20, divided into three apartments; all is much ruined.

This is a brief account of what Stephens saw of the ruins of Uxmal; but he also saw the title deeds of the lands upon which they stand.

The first is from the Spanish Government, dated 12th May, 1673; the second a deed of confirmation of this, on which it was certified that livery of seizin under it was made *by opening and shutting some doors of these buildings &c.*, in January 1688. The former deed recited the petition of the grantee for it, "*because it would prevent the Indians*

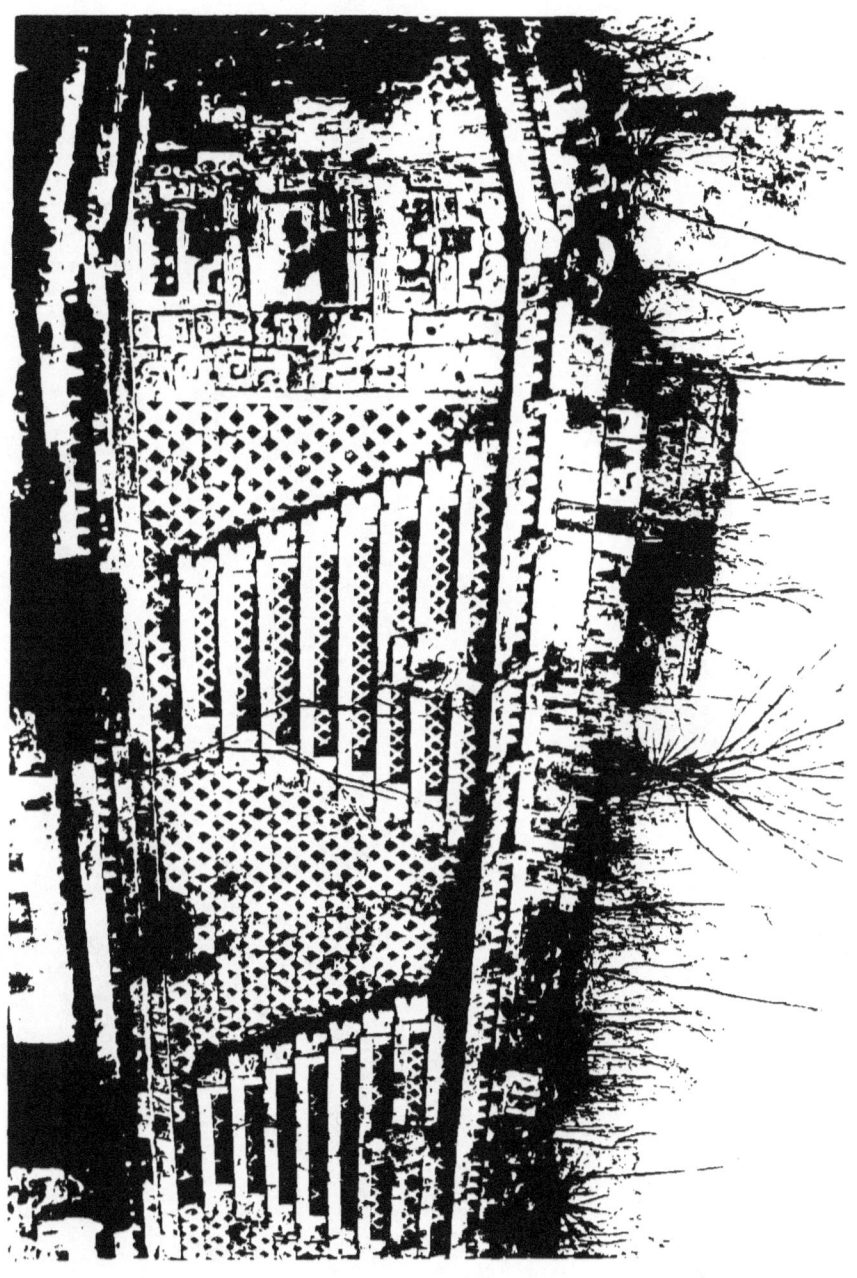

A PART OF THE PALACE OF THE NUNS, UXMAL.

from worshipping the devil in the ancient buildings there, having in them their idols, to which they burn copal, and performing other detestable sacrifices, &c." Any doubt as to what these high buildings on pyramidal elevations were used for, is set at rest by the Padre Cogolludo, a Franciscan friar, and historian of Yucatan, whom Stephens mentions, at all events, as to one of the buildings here, the House of the Dwarf. Cogolludo says that "there were the idols, and that there the inhabitants made sacrifices of men, women and children." Of these sacrifices he gives a frightful description, much the same as that at page 58 *ante*, and he adds to it the account of them by one, who had been one of their priests, but was converted.

So there was no doubt left, but that these ruins were inhabited, and used at the time of the Spaniards coming.

CHICHEN-ITZA.

These ruins are all of stone, on the site of an ancient city, and are in the State of Yucatan, Mexico, about thirty miles westerly from Valladolid, near the line of railway from Merida to that place, probably now completed.

They are on a hacienda called by the same name, and were visited and described by Stephens, in 1842. He says the buildings are large, some in good preservation, the facades, not so elaborately ornamented as some he had seen, seemed of an older date and the sculpture is ruder, but the interior apartments contained decorations and devices new to him. What is standing is principally :

1. A building 149 feet in front, 48 feet deep, with a grand staircase 45 feet wide in the centre, to the roof of this building, in which are 18 apartments.

At the south end is a chamber, in which is a sculptured figure in stone which has been painted in red, blue, and yellow, and above are *hieroglyphics sculptured in stone, which*, he says, *beyond all question bore the same type with those at Copan and Palenque.*

2. A long majestic pile named, like that at Uxmal, the Palace of the Nuns, composed of two structures, one a wing to the other : the whole length is 228 feet, the main or principal front 112 feet ; this seems to be of solid masonry, a solid structure, the wing only having chambers. A grand staircase 32 feet high and 56 feet wide rises to the top, having 39 steps. On the top stands a range of buildings with a platform 14 feet in front extending all round them. For further description of this building and of the others, where I am deficient in it, I must refer to Stephens' book.

3. What is known as the Eglesia or Church, which is 26 feet by 14 feet, and 31 feet high, with two cornices, elaborate and rich in design. Over the doorway is a range of hieroglyphics, and above these stand out in bold relief, six projecting carved ornaments in stone, which as

at the Governor's Palace, at Uxmal, he likens to elephants' trunks. but I do not see much resemblance to them. If they were so intended, where did the builder get them from?

4. A circular building called the Caracol or winding staircase. It stands on the upper of two terraces, the lower one 223 feet by 150 feet, the upper 80 feet by 55.

A grand staircase 45 feet wide rises to the platform of the lower terrace, and on each side is a balustrade with the entwined bodies of two gigantic serpents, three feet wide, parts of which were still in position; and among the ruins, at the foot of the staircase, one immense head remains.

The platform of the upper terrace is 80 feet by 65, and is reached by another staircase 42 feet wide, with 16 steps, on the last of which stands this circular building.

It is 22 feet in diameter and has four small doorways facing the cardinal points. Above, the cornice has fallen a good deal, and the roof slopes so as almost to form a point.

The height, with the terraces, is about 60 feet. Stephens said of this building, " it drew closer the curtain that already shrouded these mysterious structures."

5. An edifice with two immense parallel walls, each 274 feet long, 30 thick, and 120 feet apart. In the centre of the great stone walls opposite each other, and twenty feet from the ground, are two massive stone rings, with a rim and border of two sculptured entwined serpents. The diameter of each hole left in the walls ornamented by these rings is one foot seven inches. Stephens called this and a similar building found by him at Uxmal, gymnasiums, or tennis courts, from their being similar to a structure in the city of Mexico, described by Herrara; who says that Montezuma took much delight in seeing sport at ball in it, which the Spaniards soon prohibited. The ball was made of what could only be india rubber, and of those who played, he that sent it through one of these holes won.

This ruined building, Stephens says, " draws together the people of the city of Mexico, and those of Yucatan; and alluding to a drawing of the Stone of Sacrifice in the Museum of Mexico already mentioned, he says, that the sculptures in the walls of a ruinous building described by him, near the tennis court, though differing in detail, are of the same general character with those sculptured on this stone.

But the building most visible in Chichen is what is called the Castillo. The ruins are much resorted to on a Sunday by the neighbouring villagers of Pistè; and the picturesque effect of this building is much added to by their presence.

The mound or pyramid on which it is placed is on the north and and south sides 197 feet, on the others 202. It is built up from the plain to the height of 75 feet.

On the ground, at the foot of the main staircase, are two colossal serpents' heads in stone, ten feet long.

The platform on the top is 61 feet by 64, and the building on it is 43 feet by 49.

There are doorways with sapote lintels and piers and elaborate sculpture and inside an apartment 13 feet wide by 17 high in which are two square pillars with sculptured figures on them.

But from the lofty height of this chamber Stephens saw on the ground below, groups of small columns, which, on examination, he says, were found to stand in rows of three, four, and five abreast, many rows continuing in the same direction, when they were changed and pursued another.

All were low, many only three feet high ; the highest not more than six feet ; and they consisted of several separate pieces like millstones. Many of them have fallen, all in the same direction, as if thrown down intentionally. In some places they extended to the bases of large mounds on which were ruined buildings and fragments of sculpture ; in others they branched off and terminated abruptly. Stephens counted 380 of them, and there were many more. He could not make out— who can ?—what they were intended for.

MERIDA.

The site of this city was covered before it existed, with ancient structures. In one of the lower cloisters of the old Franciscan Convent there are two parallel corridors ; and the outer one, Stephens says, has that peculiar arch he so often met with, "two sides rising to meet each other, and covered when within a foot of forming an apex by a flat layer of stones."

The Spaniards had doubtless made use of this part of an old pagan building, which they found standing and sound, in the construction of this corridor. This was seen and noted by Stephens, and tended to confirm a conclusion previously formed by him, and given to the world in both his books ; a conclusion more and more confirmed by his researches in Yucatan afterwards, a very small part of which only I have noted.

He speaks in his last work, vol. 2, p. 444, of having discovered the "remains of forty-four ancient cities there, most of them but a short distance apart ; with but few exceptions all were lost, buried and unknown ; some of them, perhaps, never looked upon by the eyes of a white man." Among these, he describes and gives the following in his book, many of them with plates. All are easy of access from Merida, which is easy of access from New York and New Orleans, &c. Mayapan, Ticol, Nohcacab, Kabah, Zayi, Sabach, Labnah, Kewick, Sacbey, Xampon, Labpak, Zibinocac, Iturbide, Macoba, Yukatzib, Zaccacal, Akil, Mani, Silan, Ake, Yalahoo, Cozumel, Tuloom, Izamel.

The reader of this paper must be told here, that before going to Ocosingo and Palenque, Mr. Stephens had visited and describes in his book first mentioned, the ruins of Copan, Quirigua and Santa Cruz del Quiche. All three are in Guatemala.

In the last named no hieroglyphics, statues, or carved figures were found ; and Copan and Quirigua were, therefore, declared much older in date, and to have been cities of a race different from Santa Cruz del Quiche.

At Copan were discovered many idols and altars of beautifully carved stone ; each was a monolith, and the idols were from 12 to 14 feet high. At Quirigua idols and altars were found, but much larger, and their sculpture not so distinct, it being, it was thought, a place of much older date than Copan. But at each place the idols and altars had hieroglyphics on them, "of exactly the same style." Each of these places has pyramidal structures, and their monuments "are of the same general character."

(For the form of these idols reference is made not only to Stephens' book, but to Chambers' Cyclopedia, vol. 1, title, America, American Antiquities ; and on the latter subject generally to the American Cyclopedia of D. Appleton & Co., vol. 1, already mentioned in this paper, and which I have found of much use generally.)

In Stephens' book some of these hieroglyphics from Copan are copied—they are *the same in character* with those of Palenque, Uxmal, and Chichenitza. In his first book, at page 454, he reproduces them (I am, by the permission of Messrs. Harper Brothers, allowed to copy them), to compare them with some manuscript hieroglyphics, published by Humboldt, which escaped the hands of the Spaniards in the City of Mexico, and are now preserved in the Library of Dresden. I reproduce both, in the plate in front of this page, that it may be judged whether, as Stephens says, they are alike.

He draws the inference from the comparison, that the Aztecs or Mexicans, at the time of the conquest, had the same written language with the people of Copan and Palenque ; and if this inference be right those of Yucatan and Quirigua should be added.

But this paper, already much longer than was intended, must be drawn to a close ; and in doing this the questions present themselves :

Who are the builders of these ancient stone and other structures, and ancient cities, and where did they, the builders, come from ?

Stephens says at p. 323, vol. 2, Yucatan, "These cities were, of course, not all built at one time, but are the remains of different epochs."

Speaking of Aké at p. 444, he says, "It is strange that no mention is made of the buildings there by the Spaniards ; but no inference is to be drawn from it, for they marched close under the great pyramids of Otumba and yet made no mention of their existence."

In this work, and in his previous one, he gives his belief, and many

HIEROGLYPHICS SCULPTURED IN STONE AT COPAN.

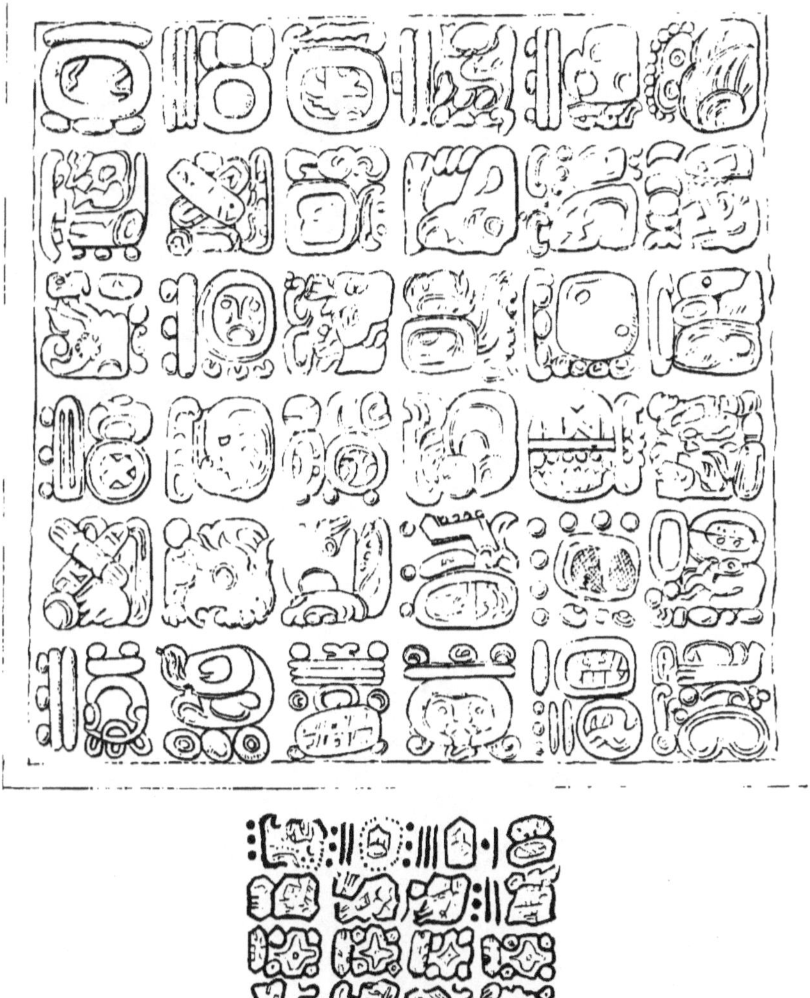

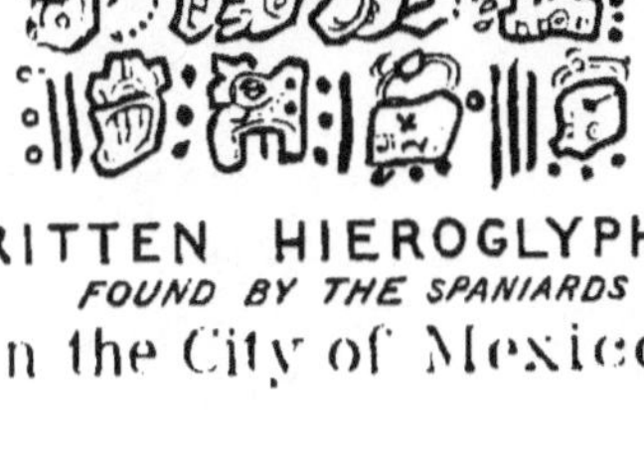

WRITTEN HIEROGLYPHICS,
FOUND BY THE SPANIARDS
In the City of Mexico.

reasons for that belief, among which is the one that Bernal Diaz and others of the Spaniards *did* describe these ancient monuments, in this and similar language : " Very well constructed buildings of *lime* and *stone* with figures of *serpents* and of *idols* painted upon the walls"—"*idols* with *diabolical countenances,*" " *high towers*—sculptured ornaments— *lofty temples with high ranges of steps,*" &c. ; and his conclusion given again and again (p. 442, vol. 2, of his first work, and p. 445 of the second work, vol. 2), is this " That there is not sufficient ground for the belief in the great antiquity that has been ascribed to these ruins ; that they are not the works of people who have passed away, and whose history has become unknown ; but opposed as his idea is to all previous specu- lations, *that they were constructed by the races who occupied* the country *at the time of the invasion by the Spaniards, or of some not very* distant progenitors."

He adds, in his last work, " Some were probably in ruins, but in general I believe that they were occupied by the Indians at the time of this invasion." And further, he says at p. 455, "they claim no affinity with the works of any known people," and he leaves them in the " feeble hope that his pages may in some way throw a glimmer of light upon the great and long vainly mooted question, who were the peoplers of America ! "

Baldwin, whose work is on a great subject, part of which only is touched in this paper, says in his " Ancient America," " That there was communication between Eastern Asia and America in very ancient times, through the Malays or otherwise, is in a high degree probable. This continent was known to the Japanese and Chinese long before the time of Columbus. But neither the Malays, the Chinese, nor the Japanese came here as civilisers, for there is no trace of either of these people in the old ruins, or in the ancient language of the country, or in anything we know of the people whom these American ruins repre- sent," p. 170.

Brasseur de Bourbourg at p. 20 of his introduction, says, Gomara declares that at the time of the expedition of Cortés and Alarcon to the Pacific " they saw on the coast ships which had pelicans of gold and silver at the prow, also merchandize ; and they thought they were from Cathay and from China, because the sailors of the ships gave them to understand by signs that they had had a journey of thirty days."

Speaking of the Colhuans, who, he says, seem to have been in some respects more advanced in civilization than the Toltecs, and were an- terior to them, Baldwin says, in his " Ancient America " : " In my judgment, it is not improbable that they came by sea from South America," page 200.

Speaking of certain sciences, at p. 181, he says, " And they present, also, another fact, namely, that the antiquity of civilization is very great, and suggest that in remote ages it may have existed, with im-

M

portant developments, in regions of the earth, now described as barbarous."

At p. 184, he says, speaking of these ruins: "The more we study them, the more we find it necessary to believe that the civilization they represent was originated in America, and probably in the region where they are found. It did not come from the Old World; it was the work of some remarkably gifted branch of the race found on the southern part of this continent when it was discovered in 1492. Undoubtedly it was very old. Its original beginning may have been as old as Egypt, or even farther back in the past, than the ages to which Atlantis must be referred; and it may have been later than the beginning of Egypt. Who can certainly tell its age? Whether earlier or later, it was original."

At p. 185, he says of them, "the culture and the work were wholly original, wholly American."

And at p. 246, speaking of the Peruvian civilization: "It may be, that all the old American civilization had a common origin in South America; and that all the ancient Americans whose civilization can be traced in remains found north of the Isthmus, came originally from that part of the continent."

At p. 221, he says: "If the country had never, in the previous ages, felt the influence of a higher culture than that of the Aztecs, it would not have now, and never could have had, ruined cities like Mitla, Copan and Palenque. Not only was the system of writing shewn by the countless inscriptions, quite beyond the attainments of Aztec art, but, also, the abundant sculptures and the whole system of decoration found in the old ruins."

Prescott, in his "History of the Conquest of Mexico," so often referred to, in his conclusion says, "The reader of the preceding pages, may, perhaps, acquiesce in the general conclusions—not startling by their novelty. First, that the coincidences are sufficiently strong to authorise a belief, that the civilisation of Anahuac was, in some degree, influenced by that of Eastern Asia.

"And secondly, that the discrepancies are such as to carry back the communication to a very remote period; so remote that this foreign influence, has been too feeble to interfere materially with the growth of what may be regarded in its essential features, as a peculiar and indigenous civilization."

But the latter part of the questions that have presented themselves in this paper, perhaps, involve this; and it is much wider in its scope: Who were the original inhabitants of this part of America; how was the continent peopled? There are many theories upon the subject, and it is only proper shortly to give some of them. The original inhabitants of this continent have been regarded, according to one of these theories, as a separate race, having no common origin like the rest of mankind; again their origin has been attributed to some antediluvians, who survived the deluge in Noah's time ; and so they were held to be the most ancient people on the earth. They have been said to come from the sons of Noah, the Jews, the Canaanites, the Phœnicians, the Carthaginians, the Greeks, the Scythians, the Chinese, the Mongols (but they are perhaps included in the former), the Malays, the Japanese, Swedish, and the Welsh ; the last from the history upon which Southey's " Madoc " is written.

And there is the theory about Atlantis, which was a large island, lying off the Pillars of Hercules in the Atlantic Ocean, first mentioned by Plato, who represents an Egyptian priest as so describing it to Solon : he gives a beautiful picture of this island, or part of this continent or imaginary land (which was it ?).

In Schlegel's "Philosophy of Life and Philosophy of Language." Bohn's edition, p. 81, he says : " Of the new world in the other hemisphere, a trace unquestionably is to be found in antiquity, in the legend of the Island of Atlantis. The general description of this island, as equal in extent to both Asia and Africa together, agrees remarkably with the size of America. But the fable contains the additional circumstance, that having existed in the Western Ocean in very ancient times, it was subsequently swallowed up by the waves. From this circumstance I am led to infer that the legend did not, as is generally supposed, owe its origin to Phœnician navigators, who, even if it be true that they did succeed in sailing round Africa, most assuredly never ventured so far westward. Like so much besides that is equally great and grand, and indeed far grander, the main fact of the legend seems to be derived from an original tradition from the primeval times, when unquestionably man was far better acquainted with his whole habitation of this earth, than in the days of the infant and imperfect science of Greece, or even of the more advanced and enlightened antiquity. A vague traditionary notion of its existence lived on from generation to generation. But afterwards, when even the Phœnician sailors, however far they penetrated into the wide ocean, were unable to give any precise information about, or adduce any proof of the fact, the hypothesis was advanced, and finally added to the tradition, that the island had been swallowed up by the sea."

I cannot refrain from adding here, as bearing upon the subject of this paper, the following surprising information, which a friend has just handed me, from the columns of a newspaper :

" Evidence of probable intercourse between ancient Troy or its vicinity and Eastern Asia appears to have been substantiated by the Chinese Minister to Germany, the result of whose examination of a certain inscription in Dr. Schliemann's collection is thus reported in European journals :—The *Norddeutsche Zeitung* says that the Chinese Ambassador at Berlin, Li Fangpao, well known in his own country as a great scholar, has lately read as Chinese the inscription on a vase found by Dr. Schliemann in the lowest stratum of his excavations at Hissarlik, and figured on page 50 of the introduction to his 'Troy and Its Remains.' The learned Ambassador has thus confirmed the identification of the language of the inscription made six years ago by the eminent orientalist, Emile Burnouf, which was ridiculed at the time. Li Fangpao is quite confident that the unknown characters, which recur again and again on the Trojan antiquities, especially on the terra cotta whorls, are those of his native tongue, and gives, as the purport of the inscription, that about B.C. 1200, three pieces of linen gauze were packed in the vase for inspection. Burnouf's French version (l. c., p. 51) also contained the words *pièces d'étoffes*. 'This vase,' adds the *Norddeutsche Zeitung*, 'seems consequently to furnish a fresh proof of the active commercial intercourse, which the people of the ' Hyperboreans,' the Chinese, carried on with Greece and Asia Minor, a commercial intercourse as to whose route the Geographical Society here have just listened to a most interesting lecture.'"

This paper must now be closed. Much that would add information on its subject is omitted with regret, as it is already much longer than was intended.

Such as it is, it is left for those who may be good enough to read it, to aid them in forming and drawing their own conclusions, where needed.

THORNWOOD, 31st Oct., 1879.

INDEX TO THE APPENDIX.

	PAGE
Ancient nations inhabiting Mexico	143
Anahuatlacs (seven tribes)	144
Ake	175, 176
Akil	175
Atlantis, Theory of	179
Aztlan	144
Aztecs and six tribes with them	143, 144, 145
Baldwin's conclusions	177, 178
Becher's, Rear Admiral, Landfall of Columbus, note	154
Belus, Temple of	159
Campeachy	154
Cacique of Mani	155
Chichen-Itza	173, 174, 175
Chichimecs	144, 145
Cholula, pyramid of	158, 159
Civilization found by Spaniards in Mexico	149
Columbus' landfall, note	154
Copan	176, 177
Cozumel	175
David and Uriah, counterpart of	148
Dominion, extent of Aztec	150
Druses, note	144
Golden age of Tezcuco	145
Government of Mexico, as found by Spaniards, &c	149
Grijalva	155

INDEX.

	PAGE
Hieroglyphics	155, 173, 176, 177
Huemac	144
Human sacrifices	144, 153, 155, 157, 173
Indian corn, nearly lost	145
Iturbide	175
Izamel	175
Kabah	175
Kewick	175
Labnah	175
Labpak	175
League between Mexico, Tezcuco and Tlacopan	145
Macoba	175
Mani	155, 175
Mayas	154, 155
Mayapan	155, 175
Merida	175
Metre, 39 inches 37-100	162
Mexican kings	145
Mexicans	149, 150, 151, 152, 153, 154
Mitla	161, 162
Mizantla	161
Montezuma	150
Nahuatlacs (Aztecs, &c.)	144
Nezahualcoyotl	145, 146, 147, 148, 149
Ocosingo	168
Palenque	162 to 168
Papantla	159
Prescott's conclusions	178
Priesthood	152, 153
Quetzalcohuatl, or, Quetzalcoatl	143, 144, 151, 155, 158
Quirigua	176
Sabach	175
Sacvey	175

INDEX. 183

	PAGE
Sacrifices	144, 153, 155, 157, 173
San Juan Teotihuacan	157
Santa Cruz del Quiche	176
Silan	175
Stephens' discoveries in Yucatan	176
" his conclusions	176, 177
Toocali of Mexico	153, 154
Tezcuco	148
Tezcotzinco	148
Ticol	175
Tlacopan	143, 145
Tlapallan	154
Toltecs	143, 144, 145, 155, 156, 157, 161
Trees, rings and marks on	156
Troy, intercourse with E. Asia	179
Tula	156
Tuloom	175
Uxmal	168 to 173
Xalahoo	175
Xampan	175
Xochicalco	159, 160
Yalahoo	175
Yucatan	154, 155, 156, 175, 176
Yukatzib	175
Zaccacal	175
Zayi	175
Zibnocac	175

www.ingramcontent.com/pod-product-compliance
Lightning Source LLC
Chambersburg PA
CBHW021810230426
43669CB00008B/703